# THE ADVANCED KARATE MANUAL

# THE ADVANCED KARATE MANUAL

Vince Morris and Aidan Trimble

**Stanley Paul**
London Sydney Auckland Johannesburg

Aidan: to my parents, Maureen and Michael, for their help and
support over the years
Vince: for Gareth and Adrian and to the memory of my mother

Stanley Paul & Co. Ltd

First published 1989
© Vince Morris and Aidan Trimble 1989

Set in Univers light by Input Typesetting Ltd., London

**Printed and bound in Great Britain by Clays Ltd, St Ives plc**

British Library Cataloguing in Publication Data
Morris, P. M. V. (P. M. Vincent)
  The advanced karate manual.
  1. Karate. – Manuals
  I. Title  II. Trimble, Aidan
  796.8'153

ISBN 9780091949969

The Random House Group Limited supports The Forest Stewardship
Council® (FSC®), the leading international forest-certification organisation.
Our books carrying the FSC label are printed on FSC®-certified paper.
FSC is the only forest-certification scheme supported by the leading
environmental organisations, including Greenpeace. Our
paper procurement policy can be found at
www.randomhouse.co.uk/environment

MIX
Paper | Supporting
responsible forestry
FSC® C018179

# CONTENTS

# ACKNOWLEDGEMENTS

The authors would like to thank the following for their help in the preparation of this book: Chris Hallam, Nottingham County Council, Tim Skermer, Richard Smith, Avia Shoes, Nigel Benton, Sue Denholm, Linda, Toni and all the many excellent teachers to whom we both owe so much. Finally, a special thank you to Roddy Bloomfield and Dominique Shead of Stanley Paul for all their understanding, enthusiasm and encouragement.

For permission to reproduce copyright photographs in this book, the authors and publisher would like to thank D. Hague, P. J. Lhermette, *Combat*, Terry O'Neill, *Martial Arts Illustrated*, N. Harvey, A. Hampson, I. Walker, K. Biggs, Noel McArthy, M. Trimble, *Shotokan Karate Magazine* and *Fighting Arts*.

Although the quality of some of the photographs used in the book is not up to that of the specially commissioned work, the authors feel that they deserve inclusion on grounds of historical interest, relevance to the text and because many show techniques and training methods in use during competition and everyday practice.

# AUTHORS' NOTE

The techniques described in this book can be performed by both male and female karate students. However, for the sake of simplicity, we have used the words he/him/his where she/her/hers could equally apply.

# FOREWORD

If you were to look back over the records of the achievements of athletes from former days and compare them with those of today, it would be immediately obvious that today's generation of sportsmen and women are faster and stronger, performing at levels undreamt of by their predecessors. Records in both speed events and endurance continue to tumble; athletes jump higher and longer and lift heavier weights.

What has changed? What has brought about this remarkable and consistent advance in physical prowess? Of course advances in nutritional 'know-how' and the vast expansion in medical knowledge have contributed to a general overall increase in health. Good food, however, and more curative drugs are only a part of the answer.

The most evident difference between the training methods of the contemporary athlete and his predecessors is that there is now in existence an extensive body of scientific research into all aspects of physical activity. Such empirical knowledge means that the training schedules of the serious athlete are no longer 'hit and miss' affairs, relying on tradition and often poorly understood concepts. Nowadays every athlete can have at his or her fingertips a completely scientific programme designed to obtain the maximum from every training session. Tremendous progress has been made in understanding how to train for increased aerobic capacity for endurance events, and in the workings of even the tiniest of muscles for the strength-orientated events. Consequently sporting records have fallen and will continue to do so.

In the world of the martial arts, though, very little has been done in a structured way to bring about the same sort of advances. In fact the tendency in the past has been for teachers to oppose anything that is not part of the traditional teachings for fear that anything 'new' will erode this tradition. With the rise in popularity of competitive karate many have feared the decline of traditional karate-dō

*The Advanced Karate Manual* shows that this is not necessarily the case. It presents up-to-date scientific advances in sports psychology and physiology, along with other aspects of modern athletic knowledge, and shows their relevance and effectiveness in a martial arts context. And it does this without sacrificing any of the traditional values and concepts of karate-dō – I personally would never endorse a book that did seek to undermine the importance and relevance of such a tradition.

I am in fact a firm believer and advocate of a

*Terry O'Neill*

holistic approach. I have supplemented my training in traditional karate-dō under Japanese and Okinawan masters with quite extensive progressive weight-training (as developed primarily by Occidentals) for more than twenty years. Concomitant with this I have followed the developing science of nutrition, particularly in the area of specific food supplementation, and shaped my dietary regimen accordingly. I strongly believe that these 'outside' influences have had a very beneficial effect in my own training and development. So whilst acknowledging the prime importance of the classical Oriental teachings, I do feel that a blending of the modern with the traditional can be very advantageous to today's martial artist.

Traditionally the Oriental masters have always stressed the dual importance of training both mind and body. This book attempts, and I feel succeeds, in enhancing this concept by giving clear and comprehensive information for devising personal training schedules to optimise both physical and mental development, and stresses the vital importance of the latter. It also gives detailed and fully illustrated examples of many contest-winning techniques, into which the authors continually interject personal anecdotes and examples from their own training and competition experiences. This adds a personal 'feel' to the whole book as well as giving examples of how these training techniques actually worked in practice.

I have known Aidan Trimble and Vince Morris for a number of years and recognize them both as highly experienced and very able *karate-ka*. Their outstanding competitive records – with one no less than a World Champion in both *kata* and *kumite* –

is matched by their ability as instructors, and they are committed to producing the same excellence in their students.

I feel that careful study, along with practice of the concepts, principles and techniques contained in this manual, will complement in a very positive way regular karate training in an authentic *dojo*. *The Advanced Karate Manual* could aptly be described as a twentieth-century approach to karate . . . and as such I warmly recommend it.

TERRY O'NEILL

Former Captain of the All-Styles
British Karate team, and
Editor and Publisher of
*Fighting Arts International*

# Chapter 1 **INTRODUCTION**

## Vince Morris

Some time ago I was asked to write a book about karate-dō. In spite of the fact that I felt that there were many better qualified than I to undertake such a task, it seemed that, perhaps by default, the task fell to me. At the time it seemed to me that it would not be sufficient simply to write yet another 'How to kick, how to punch' manual, so I decided to include personal anecdotes, observations and reflections of my own experiences drawn from many years of training in a strict, severe, traditional Japanese regime under my teacher, Asano Sensei. The book (*The Karate-dō Manual*) was published and to my amazement sold many thousands of copies.

That was that, I thought, and got back on with my training. Suddenly ten years had gone by, and I was again being asked to write a book on karate. My initial reaction was 'Why?' I had already done that once, and what would be the point of repeating the exercise? Upon reflection, however, it seemed to me that many things had changed since that first volume saw the light of day.

Karate itself had changed. Medical science and sport psychology had given new insights into bio-mechanics and the techniques of mental preparation. Stretching methods for increasing flexibility and reducing the risks of injury had been researched. Scientific studies of the effects of transcendental meditation and similar techniques had given new evidence of the benefits to be gained from the harmonization of mind and body. The rapid expansion of the sporting aspect of karate had brought about consideration of the role of the serious sport karate athlete and of the coach.

Looking back then, I realized that my own training and teaching methods had also changed radically as I had learned more and integrated the knowledge into my practice.

When Mr Kanazawa (Chief Instructor of the Shotokan Karate International) first recommended that Mr Asano should come from Japan to live in Nottingham and be our teacher, the art and practice of karate were very little known. Consequently we students accepted the regime instituted by Asano Sensei without question. In Japan Mr Asano was renowned for his powerful spirit and strong, forceful karate. He had been captain of Takushoku University Karate team and twice winner of the All Students Championship. Upon his arrival in Nottingham he immediately set about establishing a training schedule just as severe as those in Japan.

*Vince Morris*

I well remember my first meeting with *sensei* when I was a lowly 4th *kyu*. He took the class through basics and suddenly I was facing him in free-fighting (*ju-kumite*). Just as suddenly his foot touched me lightly on the nose, and I fully recall thinking to myself: 'I must watch out for that.' That was actually my last fully conscious thought for a little while, as I found myself on the *dojo* floor watching *sensei's* feet walking away from me.

I was brought round in the changing rooms by some senior grades, and went back to the *dojo* to continue. The class was now practising *kata*, and seeing that my eye was now completely closed from his roundhouse kick (*mawashi-geri*), Asano motioned me away. I was so mad, however, that I ignored him and joined in with the others. I was determined then that he would never beat me!

The results of this type of regime were basically twofold, as Asano remarked years later. The majority of the students left, but those who stuck it out formed the nucleus of an extremely strong

Opposite: *Shiro Asano*

and powerful Shotokan group. The training was so severe in fact that *sensei* on occasion remarked that in his opinion his students had a spirit easily as strong, if not stronger, than that of the Japanese.

Over the years Asano's training methods were put to the test as many top Japanese instructors would visit and teach at his *dojo*, and instructors fresh from the Japanese Karate Association would stay for months at a time to assist him. Asano Sensei's black belts were always 'invited' to practise *ju-kumite* (free-sparring) with them. Indeed, I can remember one Sunday morning having the dubious pleasure of facing four senior JKA instructors in succession and hoping that each match could go on longer, because the last one in that formidable line-up was Mr Asano himself.

During the years I spent with *sensei* I learned much, not simply from the training in the *dojo* but from talking and relaxing with him afterwards. I will always maintain that his training, guidance and example provided the basis from which I have drawn strength in many of life's difficulties. In those early days the idea of 'sport karate' simply did not exist. The emphasis was entirely on the 'way' of karate, following the classical -dō training of building a strong will in a strong body while freeing the mind from the 'unimportant' considerations of life, death, pain, fear, tomorrow . . . and so on.

During my formative years of training in such a strong traditional manner I had also been exposed to the influence of other *karate-ka* whom I had come to respect both in terms of technique and of sincerity of training, even if they were not of my particular style. Again, my involvement as the chairman of various national karate bodies brought me to realize that there were indeed 'many paths to the top of a mountain'. Retrospectively, I could see that by becoming open-minded to other methods and ideas, far from weakening my traditional style I was actually drawing into it all that I considered worthwhile, whatever its source.

Actually, my conscience should have rested easy, as the history of karate shows that what we now know as 'traditional' was itself formed in just this manner, both in Okinawa and upon its transference to Japan. For example, any visitor to even the most 'traditional' *dojo* in Japan today is unlikely to see Shotokan karate practised in the high stances which its founder Funakoshi Gichin utilized; whereas they might find other techniques being practised, which now form part of the 'traditional' repertoire, which he would not recognize.

Funakoshi Sensei's son, Yoshitaka, was responsible for introducing some of the above-the-waist kicks, and he also played a great part in persuading his father to change the way in which

front stance was currently taught, with the hips square to the front and the rear leg kept straight, as this was not really practical. Funakoshi's successor as Chief Instructor of the JKA, Nakayama Sensei, is credited with introducing the reverse roundhouse kick and sole of the foot pressing block following his experiences of training with a Chinese master.

The final, deciding factor which convinced me to accept the challenge of writing a worthwhile follow-up to the *Karate-dō Manual* was that I was in a position to invite Aidan Trimble to co-author it with me.

During my years at the Nottingham *honbu* I had been lucky enough to be included as a regular member of the team which was successful in winning the British Championships on a number of occasions. I had been selected to represent the British Universities at international level and had been a member of the Shotokan Karate International European squad as a fighter, a *kata* competitor, and latterly as coach.

I had seen many *karate-ka* come and go. Indeed, for many years it was considered a joke that because of the severity of the training, the *honbu* five-man team always consisted of four of us with a fifth fighter having to be co-opted for each event. One particular *karate-ka*, however, had begun to impress me with his strength of spirit and the power of his technique. I remember seeing him initially as a spectator encouraging us from the sidelines, then as a member of the team itself, and then as a *karate-ka* who probably surpassed us all. This was Aidan Trimble!

I need not dwell upon my admiration for him – let his record speak for itself. Suffice it to say that when, in the past, I had been offered the opportunity to become head of my own karate organization I had always refused. When Aidan asked me to help him to form the Federation of Shotokan Karate, however, I accepted without a moment's hesitation.

When Aidan won the Open-weight Individual gold medal in the first Shotokan Karate International Championship in the heartland of karate itself – Tokyo – and demolished the best of the Japanese fighters on the way, Asano Sensei himself said after watching the Championships: 'To win this you had to win it ten times over!'

Aidan is not only a World, British and European Kumite champion, but many times a *kata* champion as well. Significantly, he firmly keeps the sporting aspect as only one element in the practice of karate, sharing my belief that karate-dō is a training for life, not just for the competition arena.

To sum up, I realized that many factors had combined to convince me that other *karate-ka* might benefit from our experiences on this fascinating pathway, and I still believe that: 'It is better to light a candle than to complain of the dark.'

Vince Morris

# Aidan Trimble

Since my early days at school I have always been interested in sport and took part in many different types of activity, ranging from cricket to athletics. Although I did very well in these sports none of them held my interest for very long until, in the early seventies, I discovered the martial arts and in particular karate. This fascinated me from the outset and the hard discipline of a karate class came just at the right time for me, as I was what could be called a 'troublesome' youth and was unable to accept discipline easily.

At this time I was about thirteen years old. I wanted to train at the Carlton Forum Dojo in Nottingham, as it had the reputation of being a very hard and disciplined club, turning out the best fighters. When I inquired, however, I was told that I was too young as the minimum age for membership was eighteen. After this initial disappointment I began training with someone who had got to only the mid ranks of the *kyu* grades, and for quite a while I spent my time practising basics and *kata* in an old church hall.

However, about a year later I became accepted as a student of a black belt by the name of Brian Collins. This was a turning point for me, as Brian happened to be one of Asano Sensei's top students at the time, and he impressed me with his power and technique, and most of all by his

*Aidan Trimble*

obvious knowledge and helpful manner. Brian's teaching brought my standard to such a level that the seniors at Carlton Forum relaxed the rules in my case and accepted me as a student, even though by this time I was still only fifteen.

I now began my training under the direction of Asano himself. At that time there were two classes in the evenings, the first for the senior grades, and the second for the lower. I used to make a point of going to watch the early class as Asano would regularly bring his higher-graded students out and fight them one after another. I learned a great deal by watching these sessions.

One of the high grades that *sensei* would regularly call out was a strong, stocky, and at that time not a very supple or graceful student whose fights stood out because they always seemed to go on longer, and although on the receiving end of some apparently savage attacks from Asano and suffering badly from asthma he never asked if he could stop, even though at times he was close to collapse. That student was Vince Morris, whose 'never give in' spirit epitomized the training in Asano's *dojo* at that time, and came to form the basis of my whole attitude to karate.

Over the next few years I persisted with my training and was graded to 1st *dan* black belt at the age of sixteen, representing England in Europe at the age of seventeen. In the course of training I was to fight Asano myself many times in the *dojo*, and although many students dreaded the prospect of *sensei* calling them out in front of the class, I enjoyed these encounters and I'm sure *sensei* did too. A friend later commented that he saw Asano smile only when he fought two particular people – my old friend and team-mate Paul Mead, and myself.

Asano Sensei has certainly influenced me over the years, although my technique does not look like his. In fact, none of his top students was a carbon copy of him, each going on to develop his or her individual style, although interestingly I have become known for sweeping techniques and *mawashi-geri*, the very skills in which Asano excelled. Although I have now gone my own way I will always recognize the invaluable instruction he gave me.

Later, when Vince was the Chairman of the Martial Arts Commission and I was fighting for the All-Styles England team, we were both influenced by other systems, and other individual *karate-ka*, albeit unknown to each other. I can remember admiring Vince's enthusiasm when as chairman of one of the national governing bodies he encouraged the delegates to bring their karate suits with them to meetings and get some practice in first!

The first time I really understood that he and I shared a common attitude towards training, coaching and competition was when I attempted to bring the new ideas to which I had been exposed back to our Association and found that they were met with indifference and even suspicion. It soon became apparent that I was the only one really interested in competing at national and international level in open events.

To enable me to train effectively I had to look outside of my Association and I drew upon the help of a fine competitor from another style altogether – Kenny Johnson, a senior student of Keiji Tomiyama, Chief Instructor of Tani Ha Shito Ryu in Great Britain. Without Ken's help during my preparations for the World Championships I don't think that I would have been as successful. He more than anyone else helped me with my personal training.

During this period karate was taking a significant, and controversial, step into the world of the professional athlete. Competition in karate had been around for a long time, although initially the concept of any form of competition at all had been viewed with great suspicion; now, however, in many people's eyes competition had become the main purpose of their training. This I did not agree with at all. Some of the most successful competition karate fighters were able to concentrate on the competitive aspect, but they used this as an integral part of their overall karate training.

This concentration on sport karate did have some benefits, in that new ideas and methods of training were investigated with the result that experience from other athletic training regimes and from the realms of sport medicine and sport psychology was now available to the dedicated *karate-ka* determined to seek it out and adapt it to fit his or her particular requirements.

After training with and competing against some of the top sports *karate-ka* in Britain, Europe and Japan, I came to realize that at top levels there was much in common between 'sport' and 'traditional' karate. Of course, there are some sport *karate-ka* who are totally dedicated to winning, and cannot rest until they amass an impressive array of trophies. On the other hand, some very 'traditional' *karate-ka* concentrate mainly, if not exclusively, on the practice of technique alone, rarely testing their

prowess in *kumite* because they have such inner power that to do so – they say – would be pointless!

I believe, however, that between these two extremes lies an ideal. Yes, it is possible, and moreover desirable, for a *kata* to be demonstrated in a graceful, rhythmic yet powerful way. Should not the techniques be realistic though? Should, for example, the side kick in Shotokan's Nijushiho *kata* be thrust almost straight upwards to demonstrate flexibility, or should it be aimed at the opponent? And yes, it is quite possible to have total commitment in training and preparing for competition success. To set the representing of one's country at international level as a goal is fine. If, however, this goal becomes the ultimate aim of practice, then no matter how hard and dedicated this practice is, the way has been lost.

The point I want to make is that there should be no contradiction between training in traditional karate and sport karate. The latter should be built upon just such a strong foundation of *kihon*, *kata* and *kumite* as the former, and should offer the *karate-ka* the chance to test skill, courage, determination and *zanshin* in a severe but constructive way.

Which brings me to the purpose of this book. Because of my success in competition, both in fighting and in *kata*, it would be understandable if it were thought that my contribution was to be confined only to the sections on competition training and technique. This would be a mistake. Like Vince, I am most concerned that the knowledge that we have gained from our experiences in teaching, training and competing in many countries, and that which we have absorbed through our researches into sport psychology and bio-mechanics, should be applied throughout the whole practice of karate, and by students of both sexes and all ages.

We hope that we are offering insights into mental and physical methods of training which can be of help to anyone. If you feel that any of them can be of help to you, then we have succeeded. Good practice.

Aidan Trimble

# Chapter 2 **STRETCHING**

Every karate session traditionally begins with loosening up, warming up and stretching exercises before moving on to the practice of the karate techniques themselves in *kihon* (basics). Because of the advances made over the last few years in sport physiology and bio-mechanics we can look back and see that many of these initial sessions were only partially effective and, indeed, some of the exercises were actually potentially harmful.

Normally the students would line up, and then follow a senior in a series of exercises which usually would begin with a few head rolls, move on to arm swinging, trunk twisting, waist twisting from front stance, hip twisting and stretching, hip circling and leg stretching. This would be followed by floor exercises such as front and side splits, the hurdle position, squatting between the knees, etc.

Then the students would move around the walls and begin partner-assisted stretching where the legs would be lifted as high as possible in front and side kick positions. Sometimes *kiba-dachi* (side stance) would be assumed with one partner sitting on the shoulders of another. This would be to aid and develop the strengthening of the hips and

thighs. Following this, the class would line up and swing the legs as high as possible to the front, side and back. Then the *kihon* training would commence.

From my own experience I was never happy with this type of warm-up. It seemed to me that I was never 'warmed up' sufficiently, and many times I would find the stretching exercises positively painful. There was some excuse, in that due to cultural differences the Japanese tended to be far more flexible in the hips and legs than their average Western counterpart. As they introduced karate to the West, it is apparent that they assumed a higher degree of flexibility in the students than actually existed, and began teaching what is really an inappropriate form of warm-up.

As we travel around various *dojo* throughout Britain and Europe, we still find classes following these same traditional rituals; this is unforgivable. Advances in sport medicine have taught us many things about the functioning of the muscles. This, combined with current knowledge of physiology and body mechanics, has enabled positive statements to be made concerning the safest and

*Vince relaxing in a hurdle stretch*

most efficient ways to increase the flexibility of any given muscle group. To ignore such advances is necessarily to the student's detriment, and moreover continues to expose that student to a risk of injury.

In this chapter we are going to look at some of these scientific discoveries and move on to suggest ways in which they can be incorporated into general karate training in such a way as to enhance the efficiency of that training.

The first point to remember is a vital one. The body must be thoroughly warmed up before any attempt is made to increase the range of movement in a limb or muscle group. Raised muscle and body temperature brings a number of benefits:

(1) the muscle metabolism is enhanced through increased enzyme activity;
(2) oxygen flow and blood supply to the muscles is increased;
(3) muscle contraction and reflex time is improved;
(4) the heart is better protected against inadequate blood supply caused by sudden violent exercise;
(5) sprains and strains, muscle pulls etc. are less likely to occur.

# Muscle reaction

When a muscle is stretched to a point where risk of injury is present, the muscle spindles trigger a signal which causes the muscle to contract, thus preventing the injury from occurring; this is known as the inhibitory stretch reflex. This protective reflex generally operates when a sudden and involuntary stretch occurs, but can be overridden to an extent in carefully controlled exercises: if a muscle is first contracted and then relaxed, it can be stretched to a point beyond which this inhibitory response would have been triggered by an involuntary stretch.

The overriding capability seems to be due to the operation of Golgi tendon organs found at the end of muscle fibres and tendons. If a muscle is stretched for longer than approximately 6 seconds, these organs send sensory impulses to the cerebellum which, in turn, sends back motor impulses which cause a relaxation response in the muscle. As the messages from the Golgi tendon organs override those coming from the muscle spindles, the initial reflex contraction is therefore followed by a reflex relaxation.

This response – the inverse stretch reflex – lies at the heart of static stretching, and that called proprioceptive neuro-muscular facilitation (PNF). Evidence from laboratory research indicates that contrary to general belief, when a relaxed muscle is stretched practically all of the resistance to the stretch comes not from the muscle fibres themselves but from the sheathing and connective tissues within and around the muscles. Connective tissue is composed of material which allows it either to recover from the stretch or to retain the permanently stretched state.

To increase flexibility it is necessary to concentrate on the type of stretching exercises which directly bring about the permanent deformation of the tissues (always bearing in mind that taken to the extreme, or done at too early an age, this could lead to undesirable hypermobility in the affected joint). Research makes it quite clear that the safest and greatest improvements in flexibility are gained from slowly stretching tissue which has been thoroughly warmed, and then holding the stretched position for a determined period.

# Types of stretching

There are basically three types of stretching exercises: static, ballistic and PNF.

## Static

(otherwise described as slow or passive)

In this type of exercise the muscle is held at its maximum stretch position for longer than 6 to 8 seconds, thus allowing operation of the Golgi tendon organs' response (the inverse stretch reflex). This relaxation response allows the muscle to be further stretched to a greater degree without causing damage to muscle fibre or connective tissue.

The stretched position should be held just at the point below pain and for a period of at least 30 seconds. Although there is no consensus of opinion as to the optimum time to hold a stretch, the balance of judgement is at least 10 seconds to ensure the operation of the inverse stretch reflex, and the general view seems to be that each exercise should be repeated three or four times and held for 30 seconds each time. It is important to remember not to bounce in this type of stretch, and to come out of the stretch slowly.

Partner-assisted static stretching is successful only when you can have complete confidence in your partner, so that you can relax and allow the stretch to be full and complete. Any nervousness will translate into muscle tension, and this will directly influence the effectiveness of the exercise. Using a partner allows you to increase the degree of stretch beyond that which is normally achieved. The assisting partner has to assume a high degree of responsibility for the stretching partner's safety, and must be sensitive to reactions which would indicate danger.

In general you should try to approach partner-assisted stretching in a systematic manner.

(1) Before beginning the assisted stretch get into the initial position and allow the body to reach its natural gravity-assisted limit.
(2) Calm the breathing and encourage the body to relax and settle even more into the stretched position.
(3) The assisting partner can then follow the prearranged assisting movements, slowly, while the stretching partner breathes slowly and calmly, keeping the stretched body part fully relaxed.
(4) During the routine the assisting partner must keep aware of the changing responses of his or her partner's body, sensing any sudden tension in the limb, any catch in the breathing, and any spasm or facial grimace. The routine must immediately be halted and the stretch cease should any of these occur, otherwise injury may ensue or at the least the stretching partner's confidence will be undermined, tension will increase, and the whole exercise become ineffective.
(5) The stretch may be continued only when the breathing has once more become regular and calm and the body completely relaxed.

**Remember: the assisting partner must work to the limits of the stretching partner, not his own judgement of them.**

## Ballistic

(otherwise termed 'bouncing' or 'dynamic' stretching)

This type of stretching involves a bouncing or jerking movement to give a series of quick pulls to the resistant muscle and connective tissue. It cannot be recommended as a method of gaining an increase in mobility and range of movement.

From a reading of the introductory explanation, it will be obvious that the continuous short jerking of the muscle fibres only results in bringing into operation the stretch reflex, thus forestalling any possibility of an increase in stretch, while being of too short a duration to evoke the inverse stretch reflex to override this inhibition. There is also evidence that this type of stretching can induce muscle soreness and therefore decrease the degree of flexibility.

Ballistic exercises within the normal range of movements can, however, be effectively incorporated into a warming-up programme, but it must be recognized that their purpose is different – here it is to increase muscle temperature, not to increase muscle and tendon length.

## Proprioceptive neuro muscular facilitation (PNF)

Originally developed in the 1940s for the treatment of patients suffering from neuro-muscular disorders, PNF stretching makes use of the relaxation response generated by the Golgi tendon organs.

In simple terms the relaxed muscle should slowly be stretched to its maximum length (static stretching with or without a partner). At this point the muscle should be contracted strongly and this contraction held for at least 6 to 8 seconds. Now the relaxation response should begin to operate, and should be aided by a positive conscious relaxation and exhalation of breath. After this 6 to 8 second period the muscle can be stretched further. This procedure should be carried out until just below the pain threshold, and held for a further period of 20 to 30 seconds.

*Karate-ka* must realize that increasing flexibility is a long and gradual process, and avoid the temptation of bouncing. Static stretching is the answer, but it cannot be rushed! Exercises to increase flexibility should be carried out at least four to five times a week. Exercises to maintain flexibility may be carried out once or twice a week.

During a long stretching session, especially in a cold climate, it should be remembered that muscle efficiency is enhanced by an increase in muscle temperature; it may be necessary, therefore, to intersperse the stretching exercises with aerobic-type exercises to maintain the body warmth.

Remember that at no time should the objective be to place excessive stress on the joints. This could lead, especially in young people, to over-stretching the ligaments, which in turn can result in permanent joint instability and may indeed be so disabling as to require surgical correction.

In the following section we give a series of exercises and explanatory notes which we believe, if carried out according to the instructions, are safe and effective. It will pay dividends to re-read the preceding section and re-think your own flexibility training accordingly. Do remember also that it is beneficial to stretch within the normal range of movements after a training session, as this will facilitate the dispersal of the waste products within the muscles and help alleviate muscle stiffness and soreness.

*Vince incorporating stretching in circuit training*

Remember too to distinguish between the type of stretching that you do both before and after a contest or a training session, this being to warm and loosen up the body in order to allow the *karate-ka* to stretch to his current limits or to relax and reduce muscle soreness, and that which is undertaken in order to extend and improve upon these current limits, which should be a specific dedicated session in itself.

# Vital points

(1) The body must be thoroughly warm before commencing stretching exercises.

(2) All stretches should be smooth and gentle and not the cause of pain.

(3) The breathing must be calm and the body relaxed, especially in the final position.

(4) The assisting partner must always be aware of the stretching partner's reactions.

(5) Breathe out as you increase the stretch.

(6) Practise until you can hold each stretch comfortably for up to 30 seconds.

# The exercises

The following programme includes exercises to warm up the body tissues thoroughly and to increase the blood flow and heart rate. Light stretching is incorporated, but should be carried out only to the body's current limits and should be regarded as 'loosening up' prior to the aerobic section, rather than as stretching proper.

The warm-up sequence of exercises should be carried out smoothly and rhythmically, and both these and the initial light stretches should cause no discomfort whatsoever. The exercises should be repeated 10 to 15 times each, or as often as you feel necessary to promote the desired effect.

*Aidan's stretching routine on Central TV*

## 1  Neck

Stand erect, hands by your sides (a). Pull the chin slowly down to touch the chest, then stretch the head back until you look at the ceiling (b). Next, keeping your head to the front, slowly lower one ear to the shoulder and then to the other side (c).

Again keeping the head erect, slowly turn to look first over one shoulder, then the other (d).

Finally, roll the head in a large circle, taking care not to force it too far to the rear. Again, it is important that you do this exercise slowly (e, f).

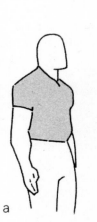

a  b  c  d  e  f

## 2 Shoulders

Stand erect and shrug both shoulders up to your ears and down again (a, b).

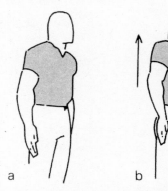

Legs apart, leaning slightly forward, raise both elbows keeping the fists close to your shoulders, and rotate both arms in a large circle (c, d).

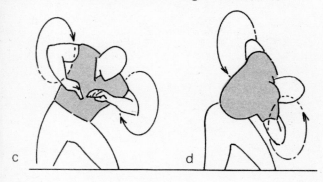

Keeping the same stance but with your hands on your thighs, raise first one shoulder to your ear, then the other. Simultaneously extend your upper body in the same direction as the raised shoulder (e, f).

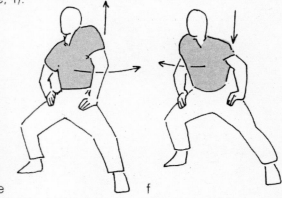

Raising one elbow, place the hand behind the neck and with the other hand push down on the raised elbow (g).

## 3 Wrists

Holding one forearm, rotate the hand clockwise and anti-clockwise (a).

Placing one hand on the back of the other, bend the hand so that the fingers are pressed towards the forearm (b).

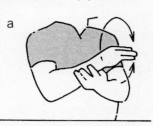

Then, holding the fingers, bend the hand in the other direction (c).

Palms together, push both wrists downwards (d).

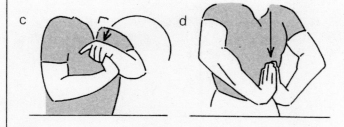

## 4 Fingers

Fingertips touching, fingers apart, push the palms together (a, b).

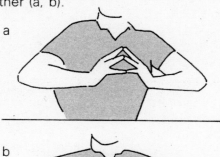

## 5 Elbows

Supporting the upper arm, rotate the forearm in large circles clockwise and anti-clockwise (a).

## 6 Trunk

Legs apart, hands on hips, rotate the hips in large circular motions in both directions (a, b).

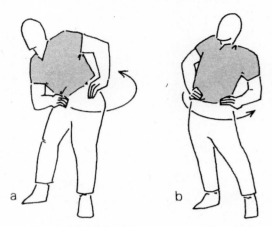

Keep the same stance, clasp your hands and bring the elbows up to the front, making sure that you keep the shoulders down. Twist to the right, then the left (c, d).

Feet together, hands clasped over your head, stretch first to the right, then to the left (e).

Feet wide apart, touch the toes of one foot with the opposite hand, then repeat with the other hand and foot (f).

Stand with your back to a wall (or support). Keeping your hips to the front, turn and place both hands on the wall. Repeat on the other side (g, h).

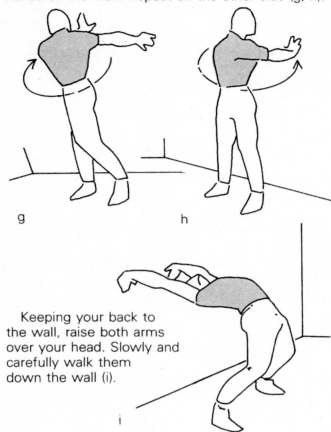

Keeping your back to the wall, raise both arms over your head. Slowly and carefully walk them down the wall (i).

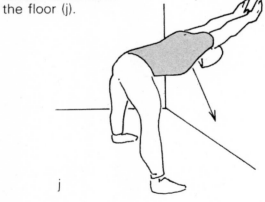

Face the wall, legs apart, and place your hands on the wall, keeping them close together. Making sure that you do not bend the knees, lower your shoulders towards the floor (j).

## 7 Knees

Feet together, hands on the knees, circle your bent knees first in one direction, then the other (a).

# 8 Legs

Place your hands on the wall (or some support). Lift one knee as high as you can and keeping it there extend the leg in roundhouse kick action, smoothly and rapidly, for as long as you can maintain the high knee position (a, b).

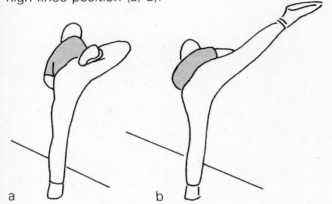

a    b

Place one foot on the wall (or support) in a high front kick position and keeping your arm inside the raised knee, bend the leg lower and your upper body towards the wall (c, d).

c    d

Standing away from the wall, place both hands on it and lean forward. Keeping one leg straight, with the heel pressing into the floor to stretch the calf, lift the heel of the other leg. Alternate in a walking motion (e).

e

Place your hands on the wall, and with one foot in front of the other, swing it in a large pendulum motion (g, h).

f    g

With your hands on the wall, assume a front stance and slowly bringing the hips back straighten your front knee to stretch the hamstrings (i, j).

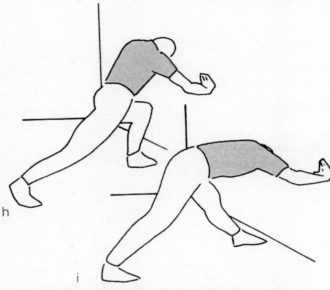

h    i

Turn sideways to the wall, and with your leg in a side kick position place your foot as high up the wall as possible. Hold this position for a few moments and then repeat while gradually increasing the height (k).

Legs apart, squat down and grasp your feet while keeping the elbows on the inside of the knees. Slowly push the knees apart and hold (l).

j    k

## THE WARM-UP

### 9 Light jog

Begin by jogging gently on the spot, keeping the toes on the ground. After a few minutes increase the pace and the height of the knee lift (a).

a

### 10 Knee lifts

In a skipping rhythm alternately raise one knee to the opposite elbow (a).

a

### 11 Jumping Jacks

Stand feet together, hands by your sides. Rhythmically jump, opening the legs and raising the arms to the side (a, b).

a          b

Next, repeat the same leg action but cross the arms above your head (c, d).

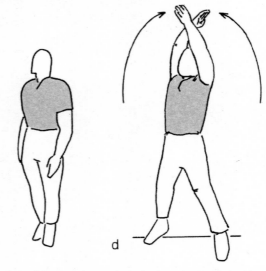

c          d

Again with the same leg action, but raise the arms in front (e, f).

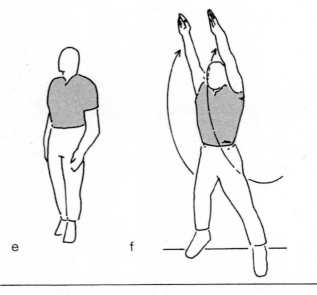

e          f

### 12 Alternate stride jumps

With one leg in front of the other, and with the opposite hand in front, alternately jump into the opposite position and back (a).

a

## 13 Star jumps

Start in a squat position and jump high into the air, opening the arms and legs, land back in the squat position and repeat (a, b).

## 14 Mountain climbers

Assume a press-up position with one foot forward, knee up. Maintain the hand position and bring up the extended leg while thrusting the bent leg straight. Repeat rhythmically (a, b).

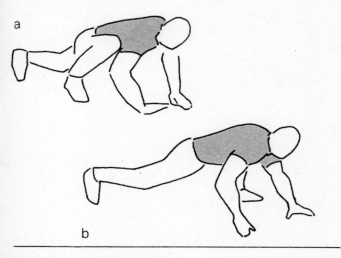

## 15 Squat thrusts

Keep the same hand position, but this time bend and straighten both legs together (b, c).

## 16 Burpees

Stand erect, feet together. Squat down, execute a squat thrust and regain upright stance immediately. Repeat rhythmically (a, b, c, d, e).

## 17 Abdominals

Lie on your back, the knees bent, heels on the floor, and arms forward. Tensing the abdominals, raise the upper body from the floor so as to maintain the tension, then back to first position and repeat (a).

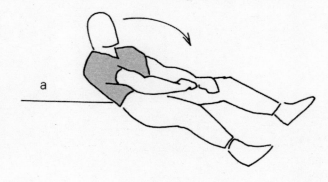

## STRETCHING

Remember that all these stretching exercises should be carried out after having carefully read the preceding chapter, and should always be done slowly.

18 Stand with your feet close together and your hands clasped behind your back. Bend forward from the waist, and maintaining this position, keep one leg straight while bending the other. Alternate this action rhythmically (a, b).

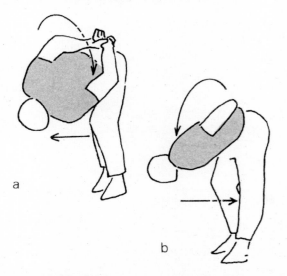

19 Feet in the same position, squat down clasping your hands behind your ankles. Keep your chest pressed tightly against your knees and slowly lift your buttocks until your knees are straight (a, b, c).

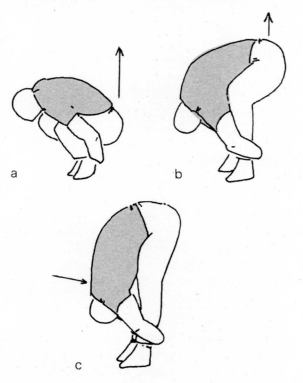

20 Feet together, drop forward so that the palms of your hands are on the floor, then alternately bend and straighten the knees to stretch the Achilles tendons, hamstrings and calf muscles (a, b).

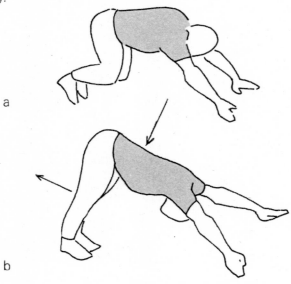

21 Maintaining the same position, alternately bend and straighten the legs, pushing the heel into the floor to stretch the calf muscle (a, b).

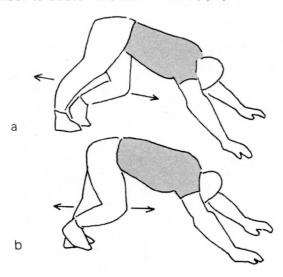

22 Legs wide apart, bend your knees and place your hands on the floor in front of you. Keeping your head and shoulders down, slowly straighten your legs, pushing your buttocks to the ceiling to stretch the hamstrings (a, b).

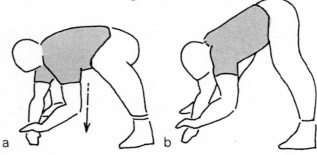

23　Assume a front stance position, pushing the hips forward and keeping only the toes of the rear foot on the ground. Then bend your rear leg until the knee touches the floor, grasp your ankle and pull your heel to your buttocks to stretch the quadriceps. Repeat on the other side (a, b, c).

24　Keep the same leg position, but this time bend forward, placing both hands on the floor and keeping your front knee on the outside. Then straighten the front leg to stretch the hamstring. To increase the stretch, grasp the toes of your front foot and pull them towards you (a, b, c).

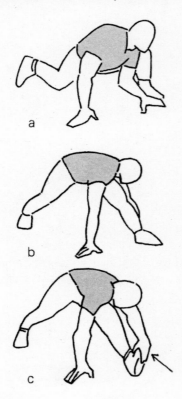

25　Feet together, place your hands wide apart on the floor in front of you, with your legs straight and your buttocks pressing towards the ceiling. Keeping this hand and foot position, push your hips strongly towards the floor while raising your head high (a, b).

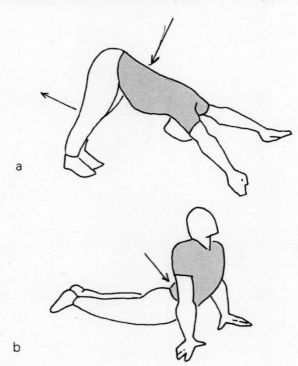

26　Keeping the same arm and leg position, kneel down and alternately arch and lower your back (a, b).

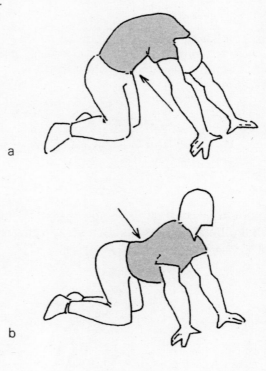

27   From the same position press your knees outwards and bring your feet close to your buttocks. Push your hips downwards, increasing the stretch in your groin. Then, keeping your arms on the floor, push your hips backwards so that your chest comes to the floor (a).

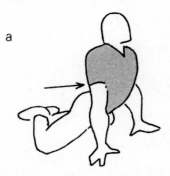

28   Lying face down on the floor, raise alternate arm and leg from the floor and hold this position. Repeat on the other side. Then raise both feet and both arms simultaneously (a, b).

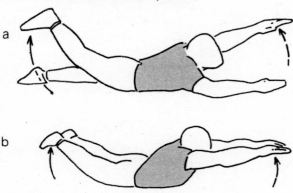

29   Lie face down, supporting yourself on one elbow. With the other hand grasp your ankle and pull your heel to your buttocks, stretching the quadriceps (a).

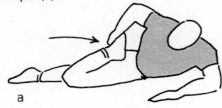

30   Sit down on the floor with your legs in front. Keeping the head up, raise the chest, straightening the spine, relax and repeat (a, b).

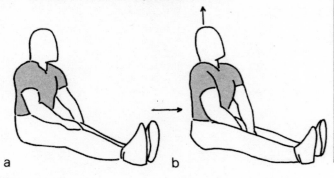

31   Bend the knees, reach forward and grasp your toes. Keeping the body forward, slowly straighten the legs. Hold and repeat (a, b).

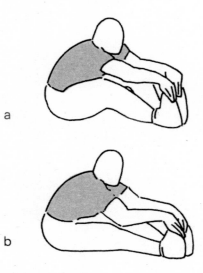

32   Still sitting on the floor, bring your heels close to your groin and grasp your toes with both hands, keeping the knees out. Again, raise the chest and straighten the spine. Relax and repeat (a, b).

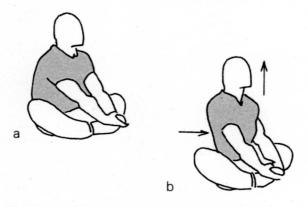

33   From the same position slowly pull your chest towards your knees. Relax and repeat (a).

34   Keeping the legs in the same position, lie flat on your back, allowing the knees to drop to the floor (a).

35   Sit up, one leg in front, bringing the ankle of the other leg on top of your thigh. Use your opposite hand to rotate the foot in a circular motion to stretch the ankle. Repeat on the other side (a).

a

36   From this position remove the foot from the top of the thigh and place the heel in the groin, keeping the knee down to the floor. Grasp the straight leg and slowly pull your chest down to the thigh. Relax and turn your upper body sideways, pulling your chest down to the bent knee. Repeat on the other side (a, b, c).

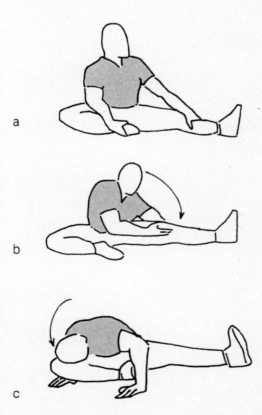

a

b

c

37   Again from this position bring the bent leg with the foot behind you into the hurdle position. From here grasp the toes of the extended leg and slowly pull your chest down to the thigh. Relax and turn your body sideways, bringing your head down to the floor between your knees. Relax and finally turn to the rear and pull your head down to the bent knee. Still in this position gradually work your arms back behind you until your back touches the floor.

Do not attempt to do this if it causes pain. Simply hold the penultimate position. Repeat on the other side (a, b, c, d, e, f).

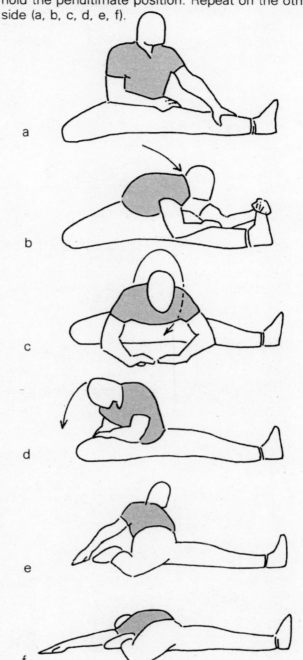

a

b

c

d

e

f

**Note:** Unless you already have flexible ankle and knee joints, do not place the foot so that it forms a right angle to your leg; keep the toes pointing straight along the line of the shin (g, h).

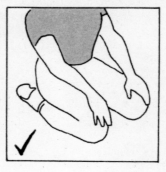

g

h

38  Sit up and place one leg, knee bent, over the other. Place the opposite elbow on the outside of the knee, and with the other hand on the floor behind for balance, twist the upper body in the opposite direction to the knee. Repeat on the other side (a).

a

39  Lying on your back, clasp one knee with both hands and pull it to your chest. With one hand grasp your ankle and, keeping the high knee position, straighten the leg and pull it towards you.

If you find this difficult you can use a belt to give you extra reach. Hold the position, relax and repeat. Repeat on the other side (a, b).

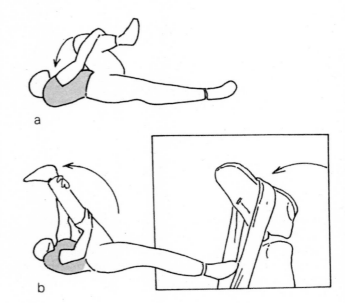

a

b

*Aidan demonstrating the flexibility possible through correct training. Not recommended as an exercise!*

40   Sit on the floor, stretching your legs as far apart as possible. Keeping the knees flat at all times, bring your chest first to one knee, hold and relax, and then to the other. From the same initial position lower your upper body to the floor in front of you (a, b, c).

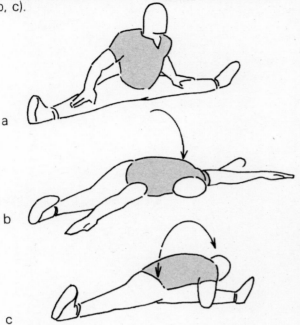

41   Lie on your back and, grasping the back of both legs, pull them wide apart. Hold this position. Relax and repeat (a).

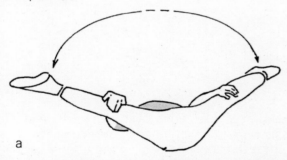

42   Lie on the floor with your buttocks and legs flat against the wall. From this position grasp one leg, and keeping the knee straight, pull it towards you. Relax and repeat. Repeat on the other side (a).

43   Keeping the same body position, allow the weight of both legs to stretch them apart. Hold this position as long as comfortable (a).

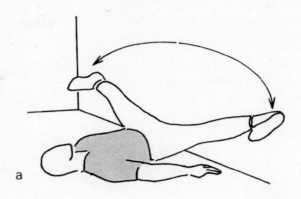

44   Using a raised support (chair) from a sideways kneeling position, place one knee on the support while moving the other further away to your comfortable limit. Hold this static stretch. Next, from this position extend the leg until the foot is resting on the support and repeat as before. Finally, twist the foot to an upright position and repeat the stretching action. Repeat on the other side (a, b, c).

## PARTNER-ASSISTED STRETCHING

Many of the exercises given above can, with a little imagination, be incorporated into a partner-assisted routine. Do, however, bear in mind the points made in the previous chapter on this type of exercise.

**45** Partners stand side by side, legs apart, grasping both hands over their heads. Both gradually and smoothly pull against each other. Relax and repeat. Repeat on the other side (a).

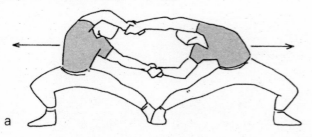

**46** Facing a support or wall, place both hands on it and assume a back kick position, with the partner supporting the extended leg. The partner gradually lifts and stretches the leg. It is important to keep the foot pointed towards the floor, ensuring the correct hip position (a, b, c).

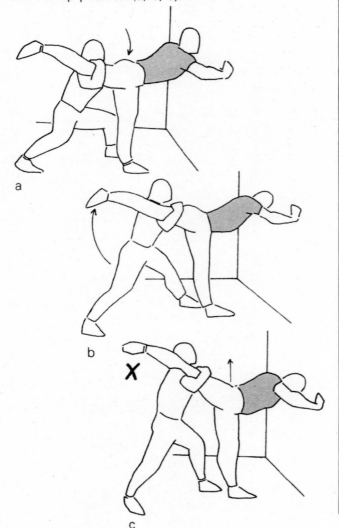

**47** Standing face to face, place the heel of one leg in a front kick position on your partner's shoulder, and hold his hand for support while he gradually leans backwards to increase the stretch. From the same original position, turn the foot into a side kick and repeat. Repeat on the other side (a, b).

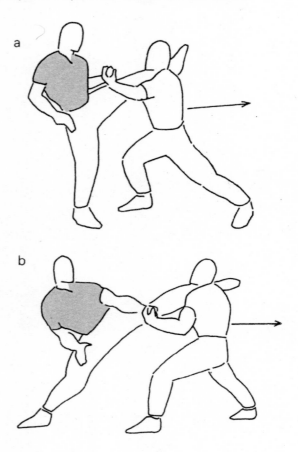

**48** Sit on the floor, arms over your head, legs straight, with your partner's leg pressing against your spine to keep your back straight. Your partner gently pulls both arms to the rear, stretching the shoulder girdle muscles. Relax and repeat (a).

49  Lie face down with your partner holding one thigh. Keeping the other leg flat on the floor, your partner slowly lifts the thigh, stretching the quadriceps and pelvic girdle. Relax and repeat. Repeat on the other side (a).

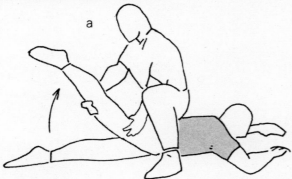

50  Remain face down. Your partner crouches down over your back and with his hands under your armpits slowly raises your upper body. (NB: he does not **sit** on your back. By placing his elbows on his own knees he can lift you with a cantilever action, thus placing no weight on your spinal column.) Relax and repeat (a).

51  Turn on to your back with your knees bent and feet together, lightly gripped by your partner's knees. Your heels should be close to your buttocks. Making sure that you keep your back flat on the floor at all times, allow your partner's weight to press your knees slowly down to the floor. Relax and repeat (a, b).

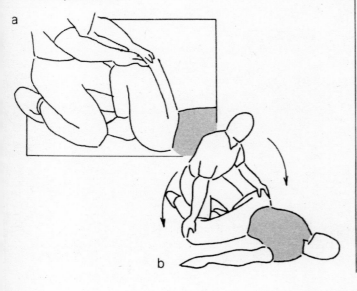

52  Remain on your back and keep one leg straight while the other is bent and the foot placed on your partner's lower abdomen. Keeping the extended leg straight, allow your partner's weight to press your other knee to your chest. Relax and repeat. Repeat on the other side (a).

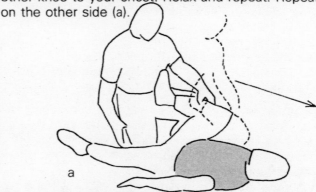

53  Still on the floor, try to keep your shoulders as much in contact with it as possible while you bend one leg and place it over the extended one. Your partner places his weight on the bent knee until it touches the floor, at the same time pressing on the opposite shoulder. Relax and repeat. Repeat on the other side (a).

54  Sit facing your partner with your legs straight and wide apart. He places his feet on the inside of your thighs and clasps your arms. As he leans backwards you allow his weight to pull your upper body forwards. Remember to keep your legs straight and your spine straight in this exercise, and avoid pulling your head down. Also, do not do this exercise in a 'see-saw' motion; only one partner is being stretched at a time. Relax and repeat (a, b).

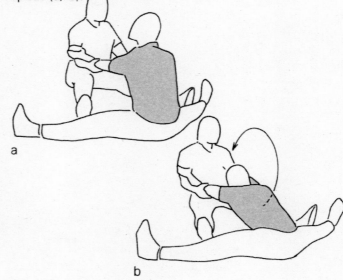

Remember that most of these exercises can be performed statically or using the PNF method. You should experiment with both to see which suits you better. Do allow a reasonable period before expecting dramatic results. We are sure, however, that by following this routine – and modifying it to suit any of your special requirements – you will certainly improve your flexibility.

The last exercise is broken down into its component parts to give you a clearer idea of the PNF approach.

55   Lie flat on your back and keeping both legs straight place one on your partner's shoulder. He kneels on the floor, placing his shin across your thigh to ensure that the leg remains in contact with the floor throughout the exercise.

Relax the leg on his shoulder and allow it to be slowly stretched to its comfortable limit. At this point strongly contract the biceps femoris and hamstring muscles in the back of the leg to push down on your partner's shoulder. Keep this contraction for at least 6 to 8 seconds to allow the relaxation response to come into play.

Now consciously relax the muscles and breathe out, allowing your partner's weight to stretch the leg further. At this new limit repeat the process and hold the final position for at least 20 seconds. Repeat on the other side (a).

Finally we would like to give a number of examples of exercises which we still find being used in some *dojos*, but which can be dangerous as they are not easy to control and should therefore be avoided. It is quite a simple task to devise safer alternatives.

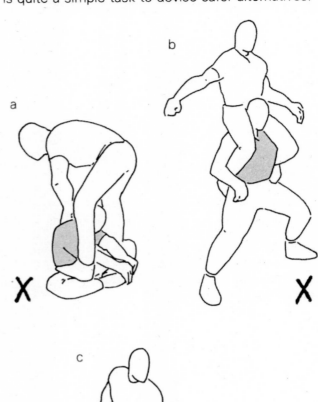

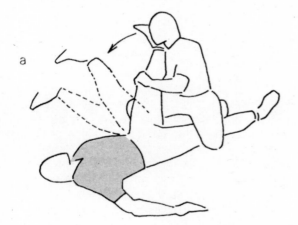

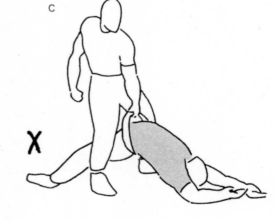

# Chapter 3 KIHON KUMITE

For an art purporting to specialize in the destruction of an opponent with one blow, it was long a puzzle to me as to why in some areas karate was so obviously deficient in common sense. Using the normal routine of practice as a paradigm, it would appear to an onlooker that all fights start by at least one of the protagonists stepping back and assuming a wide-legged stance. They would then make sure that they were at a predetermined distance apart so that they could not strike each other without stepping forward and telegraphing their intention. The fight would then begin, and would consist of mainly straight attacking techniques, and it would never end in a scuffle or wrestling match, but with one – and only one – deadly blow!

I remember inviting a large tae-kwon-do club to practise at my university *dojo* and watching in amusement as in the one-step practice (*kihon ippon kumite*) the tae-kwon-do students kept shuffling backwards to gain their normal distance in order to give them room to utilize their favourite kicking techniques, while at the same time the karate students kept shuffling after them in an attempt to close the distance to that which was considered to be their norm.

Upon reflection, however, it became obvious to me that there are perfectly good reasons for

*Vince:* Nihon Nukite

*Aidan and Kenny Johnson: basic one-step practice*

Both Vince and Aidan share the desire to leave their opponents on the floor

setting a common method of practising one-step, and for establishing a distance between the participants which would aid, not inhibit, the proper practice of a large range of dissimilar techniques.

The problem, in my view, arises from the fact that, in the main, the basic one-step practice is not adjusted to become more realistic as the student's skill increases. There is, admittedly, semi-free practice, where both protagonists move around freely before one launches a prearranged attack. There is also free practice itself. But the problem remains, for in these types of practice the techniques are still usually the long-range kicking or punching ones, and begin with the defender already in a free-fighting stance at a safe distance from the attacker. None of these offers the opportunity to practise the many short-range karate techniques from a realistic initial distance. Essentially *karate-ka* become very good at defending and countering from a completely unrealistic distance, and are taught to break apart and start again if the *ikken hisatsu* (one deadly blow) fails.

I can clearly remember the confusion in my own mind when, during sparring in my teacher's *dojo*, I would block or evade an attack and strike with reverse punch (*gyaku-zuki*). At this Asano Sensei would begin to halt the match to award me a point. In the meantime, however, seeing the opening in my opponent's defence still there, I would immediately strike again – to make sure. At this point Asano would exclaim in exasperation 'No no! Just one, just one!' and refuse to award the point.

Again, because of my years of judo training, I had developed a dislike of seeing opponents left on their feet, and would invariably follow a strike or kick with a sweep or throw. Providing I finished with the *coup de grâce* as the opponent lay on the floor, this was acceptable. If I jumped on them, however, to put on a strangle-hold or an arm lock, I would be told to stop, no points would be awarded and the match would be re-started with us both separated by the regulation distance.

Now, experience of reality tells me that actual fights seldom, if ever, begin at the distance assumed in normal *kihon kumite*, but literally face to face, or from a totally unexpected quarter. In neither case are the attacking techniques normally straight punches but swings and hooks, and indeed are often not punches but head butt attacks, grabs and knee attacks. As for the principle of *Ikken Hisatsu*, the number of *karate-ka* skilled and powerful enough to demonstrate this consistently in all circumstances could, in my opinion, be counted on the fingers of one hand.

For the merely mortal it is generally the case that a serious assault allows only a few split seconds in which to deliver a full-range karate technique before distance is closed and a grappling match begins, unless the *karate-ka* is skilful enough to maintain distance, and always assuming that the surroundings and circumstances allow this. In a crowded bar or in a dark doorway, the luxury of dictating distance is generally forgone. The example of boxing only confirms the rarity of the single-punch knockout – not just under today's rules, but even in the bare-knuckle days when bouts could last for far more rounds than currently allowed.

Why then this apparent contradiction between karate practice and hard reality? Surely initially karate was developed solely as a pragmatic form of effective combat? It seems to me that the root of this paradox lies in the shift from -jutsu to -do, which I have touched upon elsewhere, wherein combat effectiveness is no longer the main objective. This shift of concern naturally leads to an emphasis on how a technique is delivered, and on its total commitment – on the fearless concentrated *zanshin* of the *karate-ka* – rather than on the relatively simplistic concern of whether or not it stops the opponent dead.

It seems, then, that this paradox cannot be resolved. Either you train in the -dō manner, and rely on the use of one deadly counter attack, never hitting twice and never grappling with your opponent; or you practise karate-jutsu, wherein the only concern is with the demolition of the opponent.

Actually, however, it is the way in which karate-dō is practised that is at fault. It is almost as if there has been a tendency to assume that students become fixed at a certain level of ability, and the training therefore remains concentrated on the type of practice appropriate to that level. Of course, it could be that there is a lack of knowledge at senior level, and instructors who do not know cannot teach. As Egami Sensei points out:

There are also throwing techniques in karate. It is wrong to think they should not be practised because striking or kicking are easy; with only striking and kicking techniques, karate remains only a fighting technique and in this way unsatisfactory. Throwing techniques were practised in my day, and I recommend that you reconsider them.
(Shigeru Egami, *The Way of Karate Beyond Technique*, p. 121)

I now understand my *sensei*'s concern to develop within me the mental attitude and courage required to achieve *ikken hisatsu*, and I realize that by refusing me the luxury of more than one counter strike, or of allowing me to use my judo knowledge to advantage, he forced me to develop in myself the total psychological commitment and powerful spirit which underlies the whole practice of karate-do, which is to place everything on the one chance: total and absolute commitment.

It is useless to take techniques from one martial art and attempt to graft them on to another unless one is able to transform these techniques entirely and completely into the ethos of the prime martial art; and this can be done only by a master. On the other hand, it seems to me that it is a mistake to ignore the vast repertoire of grappling and throwing techniques which already exist within the art of karate.

Once a student has progressed to black-belt level he should have the right mental 'mind-set' to see all techniques in terms of karate-dō, and it cannot be right to teach students only to reply to an attack with one totally destructive level of counter, especially as any student of a -dō form is obligated to minimize any damage to another human being.

Another straightforward objection to be made is that on many occasions the severity of an attack does not justify the total destruction of the attacker. So there is also the law of the land to consider, in as much as one is, in most civilized countries, allowed to defend oneself only with 'reasonable' force. There are on record numerous examples of victims who have been sued by their attackers for retaliating with more than 'reasonable' force.

There is, of course, the reply that: 'It is better to be judged by twelve than carried by six.' Indeed

*Vince defends against a kick*

so, but surely the skill level of the potential victim should be enough to judge the degree of force necessary for self-defence, and the karate-ka should have the necessary repertoire of skills in order to apply that degree of force effectively. This cannot be done simply by basing one's training on *ikken hisatsu*.

After more than twenty years of training, and speaking as a traditionalist, I realize now that what is important is the mental attitude, and the totality of commitment. If these are correct then it is perfectly possible to adapt and add to the basic practice methods of karate – to go beyond the stereotypical, ritualized one-step practice, for example.

A study of the history and development of karate from its origins in Okinawa indicates exactly why the practice techniques, i.e. lines of students performing techniques to a count, predetermined punching and kicking combinations, predetermined fighting distances etc., have become stultified and rigid.

Initially karate was taught on a more or less one-to-one basis, the number of students of any master being very small at any one time. The students would practise with each other under the gaze of the master, who would be on the spot to detect faults in techniques and correct them immediately. But as karate training broadened its appeal and the number of karate students increased dramatically, it became necessary to develop a system of teaching karate. Now the students were not directly under the gaze of the master all the time, as the classes became too large. The students would be formed up into rows, and it became easier to demonstrate techniques from the front of a group in a class-like situation, and to split each technique into its component parts, practising each to a separate count.

Unfortunately what has happened, in my opinion, is that this latter method, a second-best method, has become the general rule. There is nothing inherently wrong with that type of practice, as long as it does not remain that type of practice. There must come a time when the student reverts to the type of training which allows karate to return to the reality from which it stemmed.

Experience teaches that many of the blocks used against straight punching attacks which are the norm in *ippon kumite* are quite ineffective unless modified against an attacker using swings and hooks. Also, since the rise in popularity of karate as a sport, many techniques which have been learned in *kata* are simply not used during regular *dojo* training. When, for example, does the average student use circular blocks, roundhouse punches or double punches, not to mention one-finger spear hand attacks or joint-locking techniques?

Once again, experience of reality points out that few if any attackers first step backwards into *zenkutsu dachi* (front stance) before launching an

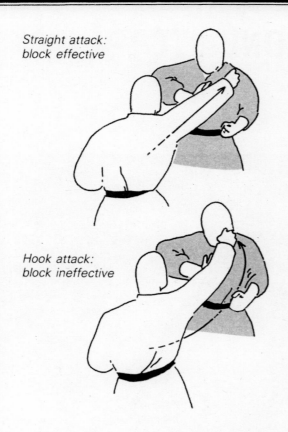

*Straight attack: block effective*

*Hook attack: block ineffective*

assault. Aidan and I have, therefore, devised (or returned to) a slightly modified practice for senior grades, to be used in addition to the regular *ippon kumite* (one-step) practice.

In this form both attacker and defender stand closer together than in normal one-step practice.

The distance between them should be no more than approximately one metre. They both stand in *sanchin dachi* (hourglass stance), instead of the attacker in front stance (*zenkutsu dachi*) and the defender in natural stance (*shizentai*). *Sanchin Dachi* is an extremely useful stance to adopt in any close-range encounter, as it is a strong, well-balanced stance with the groin pulled slightly backwards acting as a guard against knee attacks. The chin is pulled in and the head slightly lowered. It is also a good stance from which to move in any direction.

This stance (and variations of it) is practised in *kata*, but seldom made use of in actual *dojo* practice. Aidan and I both recommend that it be utilized in the practice of an advanced form of one-step training. You will find that it will enable you to make use of many of the short-range techniques which hitherto have been ineffectual from the longer-range wider stances.

A selection of suggested combination techniques for this one-step practice is given in the following chapter. You can of course devise your own, and I suggest that you take elements from the *kata* and use these to construct your own one-step training routine. You can apply these techniques in just the same manner as the normal one-step *kumite* is practised, but feel free to experiment with all manner of counters, from the 'one deadly blow' to clusters of hard, fast combinations, including throwing, sweeping and joint-locking techniques. Remember, as a rule, to strike before you attempt to throw or grapple with your opponent, and always maintain total commitment.

# Chapter 4 ADVANCED ONE-STEP PRACTICE

In these combinations both *karate-ka* begin from a close-range hourglass stance (*sanchin-dachi*).

## A

(1) Ready.
(2) The attacker swings a right hook to the head, the defender blocks with left forearm block.
(3) The attacker continues with a left hook to the head, the defender blocks using the same arm as before.
(4) The attacker swings a right punch to the stomach. Still with the same arm, the defender executes a downwards block, simultaneously striking with right close punch (*ura-zuki*) to the mid-section.
(5) Pivoting the left hip forwards, the defender continues by striking to the head with a left roundhouse elbow smash.
(6) This is immediately followed by a right upwards elbow strike to the jaw.

This is one fast continuous combination.

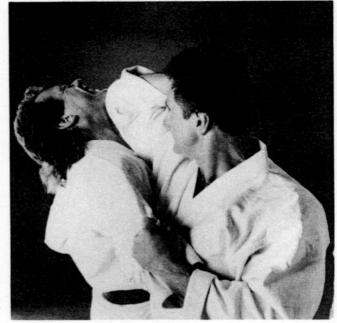

*Vince: an upwards elbow strike*

**B**

(1) Ready.
(2) The attacker swings a right hook to the head, the defender blocks with left upwards block.
(3) The attacker swings a left hook to the head, the defender blocks with right forearm, hand open.
(4) The defender grabs the attacker's head with both hands, jerking it downwards on to a right knee strike.

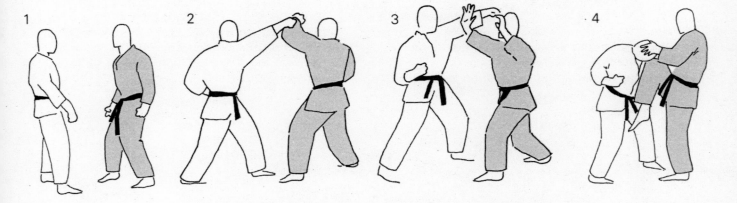

**C**

(1) Ready.
(2) The attacker swings a right hook to the head, the defender blocks with left upwards block.
(3) The attacker swings a left cross to the face, the defender blocks with left forearm.
(4) The attacker swings another right hook which the defender blocks by lifting his left arm and catching the punching arm under his armpit.
(5) Encircling the arm and pressing the elbow joint upwards, the defender counters with palm-heel strike to the jaw.
(6) Pressing the face hard to the rear, the defender continues by stepping past and throwing the opponent with major outer reaping or hooking throw (*o-soto-gari, o-soto-gake*).
(7) As the opponent's body hits the ground, drop the knee on to the floating ribs and maintaining a strong armlock against the elbow joint.

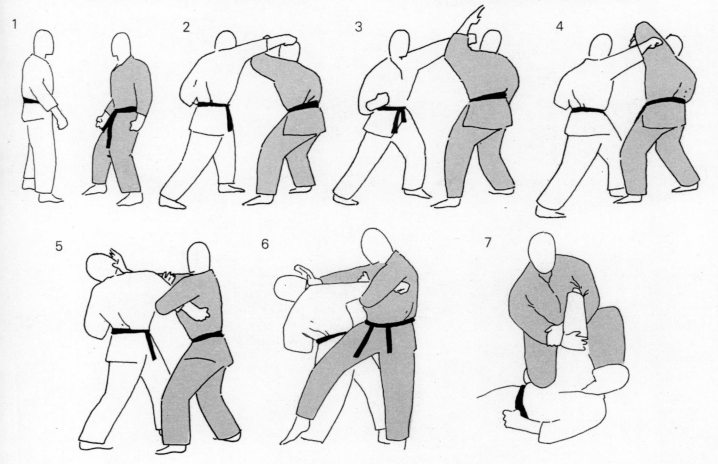

**D**

(1) Ready.
(2) The attacker aims a straight left punch to the head. The defender sinks his hips and blocks with a right upward block.
(3) The attacker continues with a right swing to the head. The defender blocks with a left forearm block and at the same time counters with backfist strike to the face.
(4) Turning the blocking hand around to grasp the attacker's wrist, the other hand is slid behind his neck.
(5) Lifting the wrist high and pulling the head forwards, the defender strikes the chest or face with a knee smash, then stepping back and outwards with the striking leg the attacker's head is pulled further forwards and downwards while the other hand leaves the wrist and encircles the arm, locking it against the joint.
(6) From this position the attacker can be forced down on to his face and the arm locked into a hammer-lock behind his back.

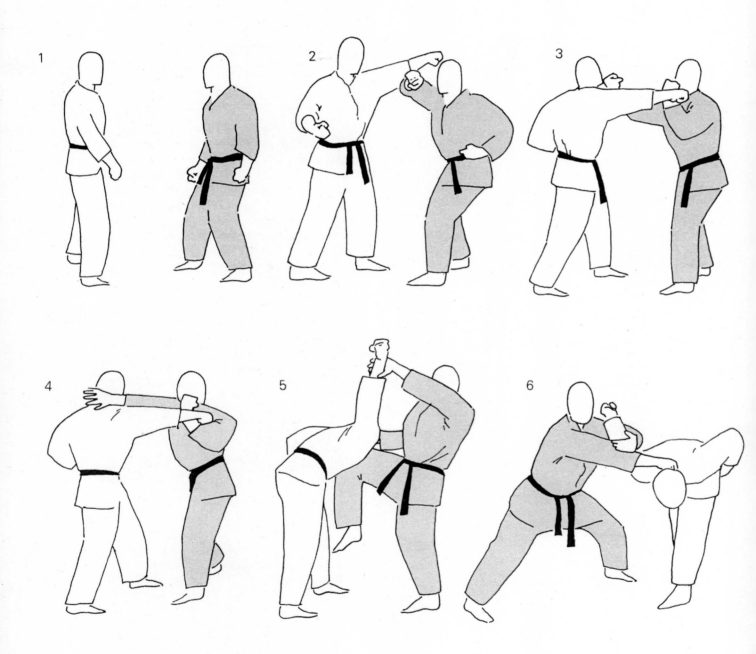

**E**

(1) Ready.
(2) The attacker grabs the defender's lapels with both hands.
(3) Remembering to draw the groin back from any possible knee attack, and dropping the head to forestall a butt, the defender strikes hard against the attacker's right forearm with left hammer-fist.
(4) This will bring the attacker's head to one side, exposing the carotid artery and jugular vein to

attack with your right forearm. (Note that although the fist is in hammer-fist position, the strike is made with the tensed forearm.)
(5) The defender immediately opens both hands and grabs the attacker's head.
(6) Rotating the hips and body strongly in the opposite direction to the strike, the defender jerks the head round in a twisting motion and throws the attacker to the ground.
(7) Finish by dropping your knee on to the opponent's floating ribs and, keeping one hand pushing down on the face, punch to the exposed side of his jaw.

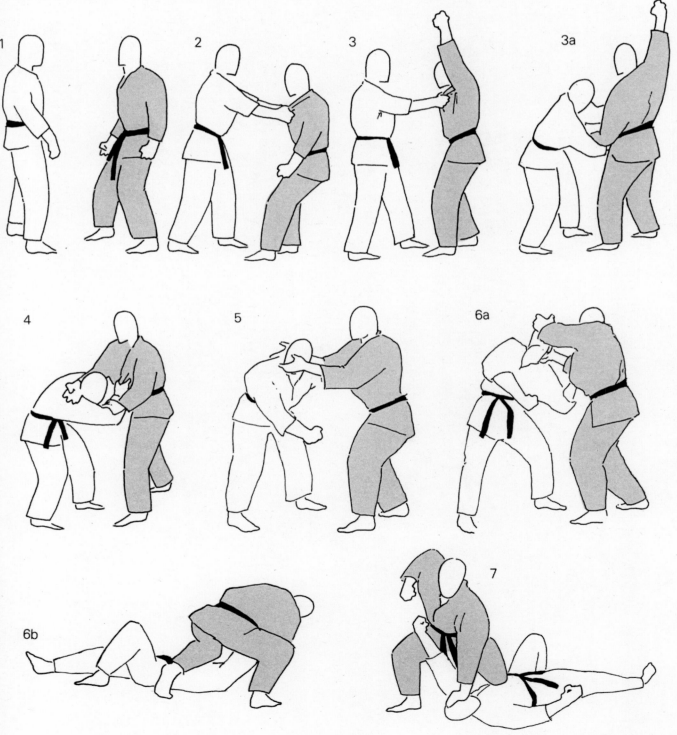

**F**

(1) A variation of the above defence against a double lapel grab. This time drop your head to prevent a butting attack and in one motion swing one arm between the opponent's and execute inside forearm block (*ude-uchi-uke*), at the same time striking his jaw with an uppercut with the other hand.

(2) Open both hands and grasp his head, then continue as before.

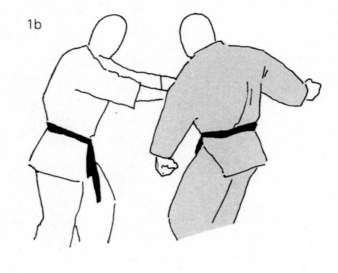

## G

(1) The attacker swings a hook to the head; block with upward block.

(2) The attacker continues with a swinging punch with the other hand; again block with upward block.

(3) Immediately slide in and deliver a head butt to the opponent's face or chest.

(4) Drop your body lower and thrust with the head whilst scooping his legs up with both hands, dropping him on to his back.

(5) Finish by pressing the opponent's legs apart and punching to the groin.

1a

1b

2

3

4a

4b

4c

5
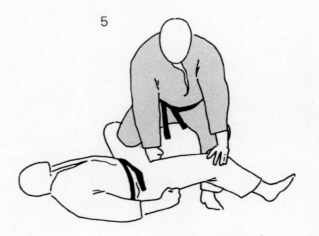

### H

(1) Ready position.
(2) The attacker punches to the head with a straight punch.
(3) In one movement, block with open-hand pressing block, slide forward and around to the side of your opponent, thrusting your other hand hard into his throat, in an upward movement, grasping his windpipe hard, forcing your fingers into the nerve centres either side of it.

(4) Keep moving past your opponent and push his lower back with your blocking hand. This will force him down on to the ground.
(5) Maintaining a tight grip on his windpipe, force his arm over your knee in a lock against the elbow.

It is important that to make this technique effective you keep the movement flowing and that your grip on his throat continues to force him upwards and on to his toes so as to break his balance.

# I

(1) Ready.
(2) The attacker attempts to seize you by the throat.
(3) Gripping both of his arms between shoulder and elbow, pull yourself sharply into him, striking his face with your head.
(4) Pull in even closer and attack with knee strike to the groin.
(5) Keeping him tightly against you, turn, slide one arm around his neck, maintaining a grip on his other arm, and throw him to the ground with major hip throw (o-goshi).

**J**

(1) The attacker threatens you with a knife and you have no other means of escape.
(2) Attack the knife hand with crescent kick to his inside (i.e. across his own body).
(3) In one motion jump at your opponent, turning your body so that your kicking leg comes down in front of his front leg and your rear supporting leg strikes him behind the knee.

(4) Continue to turn your body and in a scissor motion knock him on to his face.
(5) At this stage his leg will be locked between yours. Roll towards his head to maintain a painful lock, then release your top leg and deliver a roundhouse kick to the back of his head.

The following sequences can be practised in either *sanchin-dachi* or the more usual *ju-dachi*.

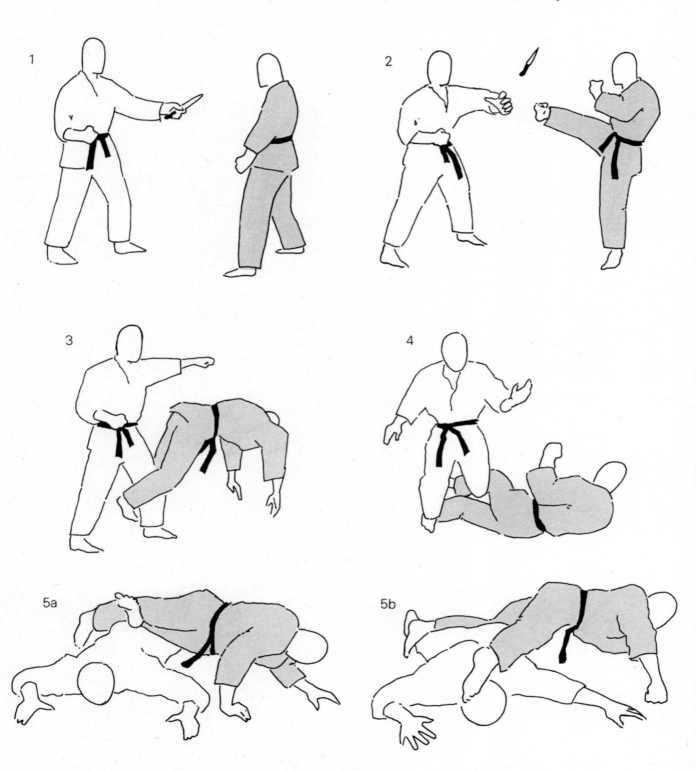

# K Defence against *jodan mawashi-geri*

Stance left to left.

(1) Ready.
(2) As the kick commences, step in and using both hands perform pressing block against the shin, closer to the knee than the foot, which will not have generated as much power as it will have travelled in a smaller arc.

(3) Maintaining guard, slide your back foot in and attack the rear of the kicking leg as it touches down with *fumikomi* or *fumikiri* (stamping or cutting kick).
(4) Continuing to turn, pivot on the front foot and attack with the heel of the rear leg to the opponent's kidney or head.

## L Defence against *mae-geri*

Stance left to left.

(1) Ready.

(2) As soon as the attacker kicks, snap your rear hip away from the centre line (*tai-sabaki*) and direct the kick away with forearm block.

(3) Immediately spin on your front foot, sweeping your rear leg deeply in under the back of your opponent's thigh. If done correctly and with speed his head will fall directly by your front foot, open to reverse punch.

## M Defence against *mae-geri – oizuki*

Stance left to left.

(1) Ready.
(2) Using the same body shift and block. In this case you do not push the kicking leg away hard enough to disturb the balance, and your opponent follows up with lunge punch.

(3) Keeping front stance, block with upward block (*age-uke*) using the same front hand.
(4) Slide close in *shiko-dachi* (square stance), keeping your blocking arm pressing upwards. Scoop up the attacker's front leg, as he falls drop your knee on to his chest and finish him with a head punch.

## N Defence against *mae-geri*

Stance left to left.

(1) Ready.
(2) Immediately your opponent launches his kick, quickly slide your back foot forward in line with your front foot into front stance, blocking with a downward block using your rear hand as you move.
(3) This must be a very fast body shift, and as soon as you land spin and deliver backfist strike to your opponent's head.
(4) Straight away follow by grabbing the back of his head and pulling him down on to his back. As he falls keep one arm in front of your face in case he – either accidentally or intentionally – kicks you as he falls.
(5) Drop with one knee on to his face and finish with a punch to the mid-section.

## O Defence against *mawashi-geri*

Stance left to left.

(1) Ready.
(2) In natural stance, the opponent kicks with the rear leg. Thrust your body at him, lifting your front knee high and bringing it close to your elbow, thus forming a complete barrier to his kick.
(3) Push your upraised knee into his mid-section and counter with reverse punch to the head.

2 (detail)

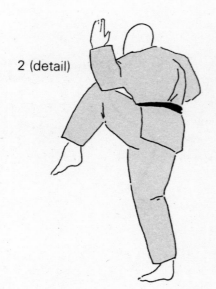

3

## P Defence against back *mawashi-geri*

This takes very good timing but can be very effective and leaves your opponent with his back to you.

(1) Ready.
(2) As the kick commences lift your front foot and execute sole pressing block against the back of your opponent's knee, stopping the kick dead.
(3) Immediately drop your front foot down and attack with reverse punch and continue by scooping up his leg with one hand while pulling his head back with the other. Finish with a kick to the body.

*Vince defends against a back roundhouse kick*

# Chapter 5 ANCILLARY TRAINING

The average human body consists of 206 bones and approximately 640 muscles of three different types: striated (sometimes called skeletal), the most numerous type, consisting of parallel bundles of fibres attached to the bones by connective tissue (tendons); smooth (sometimes called visceral), which is found in the body walls and cavities such as the stomach, blood vessels and intestines; and finally cardiac, which, as the name implies, is found only in the heart. These muscles, together with their tendons and connective tissue, make up about 40 per cent of body weight. It is estimated that the body contains approximately 60,000 yards of arteries, veins and small capillaries, and about 13,000,000 nerve cells. The average body also contains some ten gallons of water.

The muscles in the body are joined to bone, cartilage and connective tissue either directly or indirectly by tendons or other fibrous tissue. These tendons in themselves are strong enough in normal circumstances to withstand a stress of 8 tonnes per square inch. Muscles consume four or five times as much energy as they produce, and are therefore relatively inefficient unless trained. The main functions of the muscles are to support and move the skeleton and to provide support for the various internal organs. Any physical activity can certainly be enhanced by good muscular development, as well as hindered by poor muscular development.

In my previous book (*The Karate-dō Manual*) I explained in some depth the value of aerobic exercise as a vitally important factor in obtaining a good CRC (circulo-respiratory capacity) – that is, the ability of the heart and lungs to cope with the demands of the body when placed under sustained physical and mental stress. Generally called stamina, this factor governs not how frequently you can use a specific muscle group before muscle fatigue sets in, but when exercise or activity must cease through lack of breath.

I also explained that in the initial stages of karate training, muscular endurance was more of a limiting factor than aerobic capacity. As technique is mastered, however, the overriding concern is to deliver effective strikes, blocks and kicks in a continual series, without sacrificing power, balance or correctness through a poorly developed circulo-respiratory capacity. The karate training then takes on a cyclical nature: as stamina increases, so do the strength and efficiency of the muscle groups utilized in the aerobic training. As the muscle strength increases, the aerobic capacity is enlarged, and so the process continues.

Now although it is perfectly possible to continue throughout one's karate career practising nothing but the techniques of karate, it has always been the case that ancillary exercises have been used to supplement the basic training. In our experience there are good reasons for including within the basic karate training – traditional or sport orientated – these ancillary exercises, which can directly benefit the *karate-ka*'s technique.

Okinawan karate, for example, has always made use of primitive weight-training exercises utilizing whatever implements were commonly available, such as stones fitted with wooden handles, weighted jars, small sacks filled with stones, and even traditional footwear fashioned out of stone or iron. The reason for this is the realization that it is not always possible to perform karate techniques in ideal circumstances and situations.

For example, one might be on an uneven surface, or be attacked from an unexpected quarter, or be injured, or for many reasons be unable to assume the correct stance from which to deliver the perfect block or response technique. This would mean that the full potential power of the karate block and counter would not always be available on every occasion. The Okinawan answer was to try to develop strength and power to such a degree that even a technique not perfectly executed would still be sufficient to put an end to any continuance of the attack.

Concomitant with this was the awareness that it is not always possible to block every attack, and therefore the body should be conditioned and strengthened in order to withstand blows as long as they are not in a vital area, thus allowing the *karate-ka* to concentrate on the effective counter and not be overly concerned at being struck in the body. Indeed, I can well remember my early training with Asano Sensei when we would be expected to move in on techniques so as to use our bodies as weapons and ensure that the attacker's fist or foot would strike too early, thus robbing the technique of its full power and also damaging the attacking limb. Without a strong body, and in particular a strong mid-section, this would be suicidal.

I would not recommend some of the training methods, however, which were used to develop this. One was to have all the high grades lie on their backs, close together in a long line with their hands behind their necks. The junior grades, regardless of size and weight, then had to run up and down on the stomachs of the prone black belts! Of course,

*Terry O'Neill: a study of fine form and physique*

we accepted this horrendously dangerous practice out of respect for our teacher, and because we knew no better.

Happily, times have changed. What remains true, none the less, is that some sort of ancillary training, whether or not utilizing weights, has a long tradition in the martial arts. Morio Higaonna, Okinawan Chief Instructor of Goju Karate, regularly includes running in his training. Tatsuo Suzuki, Wado Ryu Chief Instructor, advocates the use of light weights in punching exercises and the wearing of iron boots (*geta*) on the feet while practising kicks. Some of the best Western *karate-ka*, Terry O'Neill from England for example, have developed a tremendous physique through weight training, and Terry has certainly enhanced the power of his techniques with no evident sacrifice of skill or flexibility.

In America one of the best of the current *kata* champions is Keith Hirabayashi. Although for a long time a top competitor on the tournament circuit, Keith attributes a lot of his recent success to the extra strength and stamina he has built up from a two-year programme of running and weight training – a regime which included specific exercises to strengthen legs, stance and shoulders. This extra degree of strength and stamina became vital when he was faced with maintaining perfect form and stance over a long period with a number of fight-offs for the decisions.

If everything else is even, the stronger man will win. I feel that is what's now working for me.
(*Inside Kung-Fu*, June 1988, p..36)

Dr Ellington Darden of the Athletics Center, Atlanta, Georgia, agrees. He confirms:

Stronger muscles . . . give the athlete greater movement potential. If everything else is equal, the stronger athlete will be bigger, faster, more flexible, more enduring and less prone to injury.
(quoted in J. Fixx, *Maximum Sports Performance*, Angus and Robertson, p. 65)

Again, both Aidan and I have experience of quite severe injuries which have at one time or another dramatically curtailed our normal practice. At these times it has been a normal and natural response to train around the injuries and also to devise and use weight-training schedules to promote recovery.

Another important factor that we have found over the years is the necessity to keep the mind fresh and keen. Constantly practising one thing day after day, year after year, decade after decade does not suit everybody and frankly can be boring at times, particularly for the top-level *karate-ka* who cannot test himself daily in the *dojo* as can the lower grades, simply because the level of opposition is not high enough. Again, the *karate-ka* at this level is normally required to teach and this also, of necessity, means that his own training intensity declines. These factors combine to suggest a rule that agrees with the view expressed by the National Coaching Foundation:

It is important to vary the exercises and training routines, so as to maintain motivation and stimulate interest.
(*The Body in Action*, Study Pack 2, p. 13)

The advanced karate student, therefore, will be well advised to develop an interest in a variety of exercise regimes which will facilitate karate development and at the same time allow the mind to concentrate on other tasks, thus bringing variety into the training schedule and avoiding any potential boredom and staleness.

Our suggestions for suitable exercises or sports to be considered as supplementary to karate training are those which promote overall body

*Joe Lewis, world champion, shows excellent body condition*

conditioning and improve cardio-vascular efficiency while at the same time promoting coordination, speed, balance and flexibility. Examples of these are sports such as squash, tennis, table tennis, basketball, aerobics, jazz dance etc., and those which tend to be more specific in their cardio-vascular response conditioning and strengthening, such as swimming, running and weight training.

As the former group tends to be activities which require instruction and the participation of others, we will assume that instruction will be obtained from the relevant coach or teacher. We can therefore devote ourselves here to consideration of the latter group, which tends towards individual practice. For the practitioner's sake – because not all *karate-ka* can have easy access to a swimming pool – we have confined our main areas of concern to those of running and weight training.

In the case of running, begin with jogging and work up to running at a respectable pace. There is no need to run long distances – two to three miles will certainly be sufficient. Regular jogging helps to make the lungs work more efficiently and to increase the oxygen uptake, allowing more to reach the blood. The number of red blood cells also increases, allowing yet more oxygen to be extracted, which allows the heart to function more easily. The circulatory system will form new capillaries and help to open up under-developed arteries.

All this is fine, but do not fall into the trap of thinking more distance will mean more benefit. It will indeed if you are interested in becoming a marathon runner. Karate, on the other hand, although demanding a good basic aerobic capacity and CRC, is not at all like long-distance running, as periods of relative quiet are interspersed with periods of very fast, powerful and anaerobic activity.

In fact, the most beneficial form of running for the *karate-ka* is that known as *fartlek* or alternate pace training. This type of exercise takes the form of a fairly long period (minimum 30 minutes) during which the athlete varies the pace of the running dramatically and frequently. An example would be as follows:

(1) jogging at an even, easy pace for 5 minutes;
(2) a fast, smoothly-paced run for 3 minutes;
(3) a brisk walk for 3 minutes;
(4) smooth, even-paced running interspersed with short sprints (50–60 metres) for 5 minutes;
(5) smooth, even-paced running with the occasional inclusion of 5 to 10 very fast strides for 3 minutes.

This could conclude with a short period of interval running where a set distance (100 metres plus) is to be run at top speed, with a set recovery time allowed between each sprint. This recovery time is individually determined and normally is reckoned to be the length of time it takes for your pulse rate to return to a predetermined level. The recovery period should be spent jogging or walking briskly, and it should not be long enough to allow full recovery from the exercise. This will help the body learn to improve its oxygen uptake and speed up recovery from the oxygen debt incurred.

There is another form of training similar to the above. In this, the type of exercise selected is specific to the sport involved – in this case karate techniques, either against a bag or in sequence, are practised at approximately 80 per cent of full power and speed for a set period. After this a short rest interval is taken, as described above, again not long enough to allow full recovery. The sequence is then repeated over the same time period and again a short rest period is allowed. This carries on for a predetermined number of repetitions.

The principle here, once again, is that the body is put under stress and is not allowed full time to recover. This parallels the situation frequently found within karate training and competition. In these circumstances the body is forced to rely upon the energy within the muscles themselves and not upon energy drawn from oxygen – that is to say, anaerobic rather than aerobic.

All the above training methods are to promote the body's efficient use of fast-twitch muscle fibres, those which consume the internal fuel carbohydrate and produce a waste called lactic acid but do not need oxygen in the process. These fast-twitch muscle fibres can produce high-speed movements over a short period of time, but the efficiency is soon impaired because of the build-up of lactic acid. The slow-twitch muscles in the body, on the other hand, use a mixture of fat and carbohydrate as an energy source but do need oxygen in the process. The waste product here, mostly carbon dioxide, is easier to handle than the lactic acid produced by the fast-twitch muscles.

These are the reasons why slow-twitch muscles are of more use in endurance sports than the fast-twitch, which are soon exhausted. As the muscles in the body contain a proportion of both fast- and slow-twitch fibres, and as the ratio within each individual appears to be fixed – that is to say, it does not appear to be possible to increase the individual's percentage of either fast- or slow-twitch fibres – then it would make sense to ensure that the percentage in the individual is trained to its optimum.

There is a body of evidence which suggests that with suitable training it is possible to force the white fast-twitch fibres to assume the characteristics of the red slow-twitch. Fortunately (at least in the *karate-ka*'s case, where it is this phenomenon which is required), it appears easier to train the red fibres to assume the characteristics of the white. The implication here is that the type of exercise regime undertaken should be carefully worked out to ensure that the correct fibre effect is obtained – that is to say, exercises for fast explosive sports, where the activity is generally of a short duration, should be preferred to the type of exercise more geared towards endurance sports such as long-distance running or swimming, where the activity is stretched out over a long period of time.

All this is not to say that the exercises should not be aerobic. On the contrary, all the above have elements of aerobic training within them, and necessarily so. In fact, good aerobic capacity (basic endurance) is helpful in that it will delay the transition from aerobic to anaerobic activity, allowing the *karate-ka* to 'coast' as it were on aerobic capacity until a sharp burst of anaerobic capacity is called for.

# Chapter 6 **OVERALL BODY CONDITIONING**

Until recently, the precept that 'the best training for any sport is that sport itself' remained the general rule. Now, however, American football players are practising karate, tennis players include a daily run in their training schedule, baseball players practise ballet and aerobics, while basketball players play tennis. There are a number of compelling reasons for accepting that this diversification is a beneficial practice.

(1) Although the primary sport must be the most important activity, other sports may improve certain attributes. For example, squash can help improve: balance, timing, coordination, body shifting and cardio-vascular response – all useful attributes to many a main primary skill.

(2) A secondary activity can greatly help prevent staleness and over-training syndromes, by allowing the psychological urge to train to be satisfied while enabling the body and the mind some measure of relief from the heavy stresses of the main training programme.

(3) It can help maintain body weight throughout the year, thus precluding the need for rapid pre-contest weight loss in order to comply with a given weight category.

Canadian university research has shown that rapid weight loss can reduce the glycogen content in muscle (the primary energy source) by more than 50 per cent, leading to increased fatigue levels and a loss of performance.

## Precautions

Although this section is aimed at the advanced *karate-ka* who should be physically fit and healthy, there is still a need before embarking upon a regime of strenuous exercise such as weight training to check that your physical condition is good enough to cope with the stresses which will be placed upon it. Do also make sure that the equipment you use is safe, in good condition and well maintained. You may need to consult a doctor if you suffer from any of the following symptoms:

(1) high blood pressure
(2) diabetes
(3) hypertension
(4) any feeling of dizziness or faintness after exertion
(5) breathing difficulties
(6) any chest pains after exertion
(7) continual gastro-intestinal upsets
(8) high temperature or flu-type symptoms after training
(9) any history of heart disease in the family.

## Introduction

Muscle consists of approximately 72 per cent water and 28 per cent protein and minerals. A muscle contracts in three different ways:

(1) concentrically – where the muscle fibres work against a resistance throughout the muscle's normal range of movement (for example, a biceps curl exercise where the muscle shortens throughout the exercise).

(2) excentrically – where work is again carried out against resistance but in this case the resistance overcomes the muscle action and pulls the origin and insertion points apart and so the muscle actually lengthens even though still under contraction. (This would be the case, for example, in a biceps curl exercise with the weight being too great to maintain in the raised position.)

(3) Isometrically – where a contraction is held with no movement. An example would be if you assume a biceps curl position and tense the muscle strongly but hold no weight and make no movement.

Research has shown that excentric exercise seems to build strength more effectively than any other, and therefore to stimulate maximum strength development you should lower a weight more slowly than you lifted it – a ratio of about 2:1 seems most effective. For example, if it takes you 2

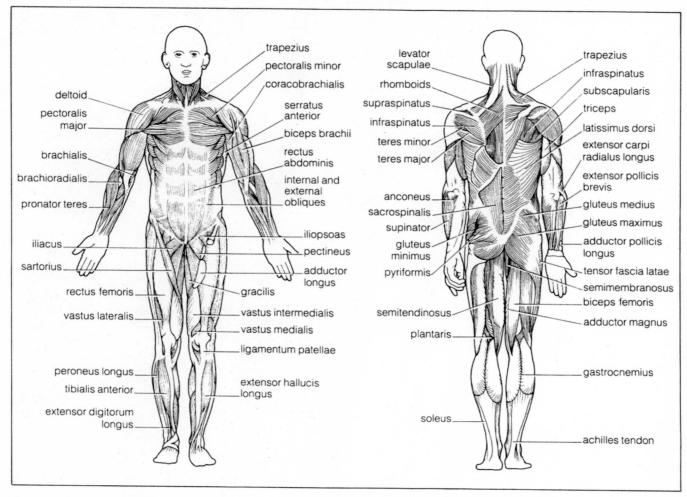

The major muscle groups

seconds to lift a weight, you should aim to hold it at the raised position for 2 seconds and lower it gradually over a 4-second period.

The basic principle is one of progressive intensity. You cannot build strength (although you may maintain it) by simple repetition of easy movements. You should choose a resistance which will allow you to complete the movements fully in a strict and controlled way no more than six to eight times before failure (with the exception of leg exercises, where a higher number of repetitions should be set, say 15 to 20).

The exercise movement must be strictly controlled because although you may lift heavier weights by 'cheating' – that is by explosively jerking the weight aloft and allowing it to be lowered more or less by dropping it, only regaining full control just before the rest position – you will not be exercising the muscle through its full range as the initial jerk or thrust will generate momentum which will help to carry the weight aloft without the full participation and maximum effort from the muscle.

Do not get into competition in the gym as to who can lift the heaviest weights. Choose the weight which forces the body to maximum effort over a series of individually predetermined repetitions –

that is, a weight which will allow you only just to reach the final repetition, and that with difficulty. Once you can consistently carry out the exercise strictly more than eight times (or 20 times with the lower limbs) it is time to add approximately 5 per cent to the weight and repeat the procedure. Remember that it is only by constantly increasing the stress placed upon the muscle and forcing it continually to work at its maximum that the greatest development of strength takes place.

Although you should in general stick to the principles outlined above, it is a good idea occasionally to shock the muscles by deviating from the normal strictly controlled programme and setting aside a session in which you use weights which will allow only three to four repetitions and those at maximum effort, even if the final repetition is only a partial or assisted one. The explosive quality of the force necessary to lift these weights and the total physical and mental commitment required can be seen as paralleling the degree of explosiveness and determination required in karate.

You must do this, however, only after you have spent some time following a basic overall conditioning and strengthening programme, and are sure that you can handle the weights with safety. If you are using free weights for this exercise then it is essential that you enlist the aid of a training partner to assist you in controlling the weights, especially as you are going to failure point!

*Karate-ka* should include in their weight training programme a regular period of high velocity training using very light weights. Hand-held or wrist weights can be used for punching practice and ankle weights for kicking practice. The reason for this is that research has shown that you should include an element of strength training as close as possible to the speed of competition or normal execution of technique, as exercise only at slow speeds adds little to strength at higher speeds nor to speed of technique; whereas high-velocity training does confer some improvement at slower speeds. Therefore, just as in visualization practice (which we will cover later) where the full technique is 'seen' at the correct speed, so should there be an element of your weight training at this same correct speed.

One word of warning. You must be very careful when using weights while punching or kicking not to over-extend the limb, thus placing the joints at risk. Always maintain a degree of flexion. Elbows and knees are particularly prone to hyperextension injury. On the other hand, using weights to build up the muscles controlling a joint and increasing the range of movement within a joint by judicious stretching can help to prevent joint injuries.

The *karate-ka* is well advised to base his weight training routine on exercise which will help develop the strength of the legs. There are two reasons for this: one is to act as a preventative against the most common martial arts injuries, those to knees and Achilles tendons; and secondly, the fact is that these muscles are the largest and strongest in the body and any stress great enough on the central nervous system to make these muscles adapt by becoming larger will have a 'knock-on' effect on the rest of the body. That is, the adaptive response is not specific only to the leg muscle groups, but also confers benefits to the other less involved groups in the body.

Before giving our basic recommended weight-training routine it is interesting to note that although the average *karate-ka* is not undertaking the programme in order to develop a body-builder's physique but to strengthen and improve karate techniques, the sport of body-building itself can contribute much in terms of its detailed research into the composition and development of the muscle groups in the human body. The top body-builders are just as dedicated to their sport as any other top-class athlete, and although neither Aidan nor I will condone any use of drugs as an aid to training, it is significant that some of their research into training psychology reinforces concepts discussed elsewhere in this work.

Arnold Schwarzenegger, possibly the greatest body-builder ever – and certainly the best known –

*Danish karate-ka and powerlifter, Sven-Ole-Thorsen, Arnold Schwarzenegger and Terry O'Neill on the set of 'Predator'*

stresses how important it is to set goals, both long- and short-term, and how vital it is to rehearse mentally a successful lift before attempting it physically:

If they fail to lift it mentally, then they won't make the lift at all.

(*Beef It*, Robert Kennedy, Sterling Publishing Company Incorporated, New York, p. 12)

Confirming yet again the importance of the mental side to physical accomplishment was the experiment reported in the *Journal of Sports Psychology*. This was carried out to try to assess the performance of weight-lifters who had carried out a mental psyching-up process before attempting a lift, as opposed to those who had been instructed to carry out a different mental task (in this case to count backwards to themselves before the attempt). The conclusion was clear:

The lifters who were instructed to 'psych up' showed dramatic increases in performance.

(Weinberg, Gould and Jackson, 'Mental Preparation Strategies, Cognitions and Strength')

The physiological reason for this apparent increase in athletic performance could be largely a matter of muscle composition. The muscle cells, some slow-twitch, some fast-twitch, work in a specific way. When you impose a stress upon a muscle the cells contract in order to overcome the stress. They do this, however, in a cumulative fashion, not simultaneously. If, for example, you squat with only 50 per cent of the maximum weight which you are able to lift, only 50 per cent of the muscle cells are working, and they are working at full power. The other 50 per cent are simply not being used. All muscle cells work in this 'all or nothing' fashion. When greater stress is added, the central nervous system generates more impulses to the muscles and more cells are brought into operation.

It seems that training enables the central nervous system to become more efficient in the way in which it excites the muscle cells, and that stimulation of the central nervous system by emotional responses to situations, or by psyching-up visualization procedures, increases the neurological output of the brain, bringing into action more of the muscle cells, thus increasing strength.

For the martial artist it is interesting to note that while it appears impossible to change slow-twitch cells – the more oxygen-efficient endurance-type fibres – into fast-twitch – designed for powerful contractions over a short period of time but which fatigue more quickly – it does seem possible to change the way in which they act so as to make the slow type behave more like the fast.

Fast-twitch fibres can generate approximately twice the power of slow-twitch, but in the training of them it is important to note that they are brought into action after the slow-twitch, because they have a higher neurological threshold, in that a stronger impulse is necessary in order to excite them. It follows then that in order to gain extra strength and to force the adaptive process from the fast-twitch muscle fibre cells, you must impose a large enough stress, near maximum effort with at least 85 per cent of your maximum load. This would again confirm the earlier suggestion that you should occasionally shock the muscles by including in your regular routine a session devoted to working flat out, explosively to failure point, with three to four repetitions while continually psyching up before each set.

To begin with, however, concentrate on learning the routine and how to handle the weights with confidence. Following this routine you will certainly make gains in overall strength. At this stage you can begin to add variety to the basic pattern if you so wish.

One word before giving details of our recommended routine. Recuperation from a really heavy workout takes up to 48 hours or even longer, so do not attempt to undertake a high-intensity routine every day. Remember that this is an adjunct to your karate, not an end in itself, and definitely no heavy workouts immediately prior to a competition.

Finally, remember to stretch and warm up before you undertake any weight-training routine. You will also find it beneficial to stretch after a weight-training session, but do not attempt the type of stretch aimed at increasing flexibility. Simply stretch within your normal limits as an aid to bringing fresh blood to the muscles and helping the body to eliminate the waste products built up by the exercise.

# Method

The method we recommend is based upon what is called 'straight setting'. The exercises should be carried out in strict form to your individually predetermined number of repetitions (IPRs), making sure that the weight is raised without cheating, held briefly in the raised position with the muscle fully contracted and then lowered to the original position taking twice as long as it took to raise the weight. The weight selected should be just heavy enough for you to complete your IPRs with maximum effort. After a few weeks, when the exercises become easier as your strength increases, add approximately 5 per cent to the resistance and continue as before.

## ROUTINE

(1)  (i) Squats: one warm-up set using low
          weights of 25 repetitions.
     (ii) One set at your IPR.
     (iii) One set reduced weight at your IPR.

(2) Leg extensions: two sets at your IPR.

(3) Leg curls: two sets at your IPR.

(4) Calf raises: two sets at your IPR.

(5) Lunges: one set of 20 repetitions.

(6) Flat or inclined bench press: one set at your
    IPR.

(7) Bar-bell rowing: two sets at your IPR.

(8) Shoulder press: one set at your IPR.

(9) Concentration curls: two sets at your IPR.

(10) Triceps push down: two sets at your IPR.

Finish the routine with three sets of crunches to
exhaust you.

Initially the routine should be carried out three times
a week with at least one day between sessions to
allow for recuperation. Do not rest for too long
between each exercise; you should still be slightly
out of breath at the commencement of each set.
This will ensure that the routine has a beneficial
effect on the cardio-vascular system.

Follow this routine for two months and if you have
been gradually increasing the stress as specified
you will certainly have made significant gains in
overall strength. At this stage you may decide that
you have achieved the desired objective and that
you can now devote your time to another aspect
of your karate or ancillary training. You will probably

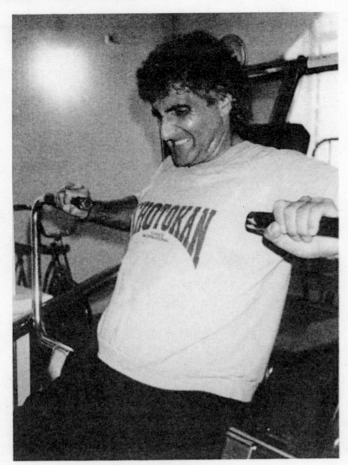

*Vince: an inclined bench press*

find, however, that it is a good idea not to stop
weight training altogether, but to cut down the
frequency of the sessions and perhaps introduce
some other exercises more specific to any particular
body part that you feel could be strengthened.

# Chapter 7 **EXPLANATIONS**

**(1) Squats:**   Squats should be undertaken with care and if you are at all uncertain as to your ability to handle the weight, do make sure that you have a partner to assist you.

Initially shoulder the weight and step back from the squat rack. Some people find it advantageous to rest their heels on a slightly raised piece of wood to enhance balance. If at all possible do not do this, as it throws additional stress on the knees.

Keeping your back as straight as possible, slowly descend into a position just below parallel. Hold that position momentarily and then using only your leg muscles, thrust your body slowly back to the upright position.

Partial squats, where the thighs do not go below the parallel, stress mainly the hamstrings and the extensors of the knee joints. Only when the squats go deeper do they fully stress the gluteus maximus muscle. Regardless of this, care must be taken not to go lower than your knees will safely allow.

Do not 'bounce' into the squat position, but lower yourself slowly in a controlled manner. Breathe deeply between each repetition so as to draw in as much oxygen as possible. Repeat this for your IPR. This is one set at your IPR. Repeat for the number specified in the routine.

Although you should work to your IPR, do not attempt to do this exercise with as much weight as you can carry, as slightly flexed your legs will be very strong. Fully flexed the same weight can be a different matter.

Do not use so much weight that you are forced to wear a weight-lifter's belt, unless you have weak back and abdominal muscles, as wearing one can prevent these muscles from working effectively and themselves benefiting from the exercise.

**(2) Leg extensions:**   Sit in an upright position on top of the unit with your insteps under the roller pads. Your arms should hold on to the sides of the bench or to the handles provided. Using a smooth movement contract your quadriceps muscles until both legs are completely straight and your knees are locked. Hold this position for a count of two before lowering your legs again, taking twice as long to lower them as you took to raise them. Repeat for your IPR as specified in the routine.

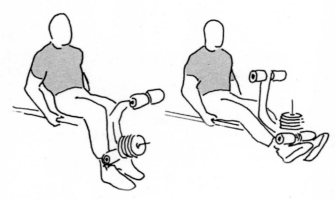

These two exercises, squats and leg extensions, should form part of every *karate-ka*'s training regime, but treated with care. One of the main injuries suffered by *karate-ka* (and here I [Vince] can speak with some authority) is chrondomalacia patellae, or anterior knee syndrome; basically, pain in the knee area. This extremely restricting injury seems to be caused or exacerbated by a weakening or imbalance of the three vastus muscles which attach to the top of the patella and act to keep it sliding correctly positioned in its groove when the leg is flexed.

Because so much of a *karate-ka*'s time is spent in a bent-leg position, and because one of these muscles (the vastus medialis) can function fully only when the leg is straight, there is a tendency for it to weaken and the kneecap to move incorrectly. Over a period this can lead to a wearing away of the protective tissue under the kneecap and cause it to roughen and become extremely tender. This injury can drastically curtail karate practice, so as a preventative measure we recommend frequent and regular use of leg extension exercises to help avoid the problem in the first place. These are also useful as a partial remedy where the injury has already occurred.

The squat exercises should always be of the partial type if this injury already exists, but should still be undertaken if at all possible because of their undeniable overall benefit. It is vital that the knees are thoroughly warmed up before this and any other type of training, as the improved blood flow permeates the tissues and acts as a sort of buffer between the thigh-bone condyles and the underside of the patella.

(3) **Leg curls:** This is probably the best exercise for increasing the strength of your hamstring muscles. Lie on your stomach with your heels beneath the roller pad and your hands holding on to the sides of the bench or the handles provided for stability. Contract the hamstring muscles slowly until your heels come up almost into contact with your buttocks. Hold this full contraction for a count of two before lowering the weight slowly, again taking twice as long as you took to raise it to the start position. Repeat for your IPR.

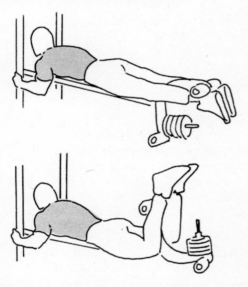

(4) **Calf raises:** Place your shoulders under the shoulder pads on the machine with the heels lower than your toes. Keeping the knees locked, transfer your weight on to the balls of your feet and press

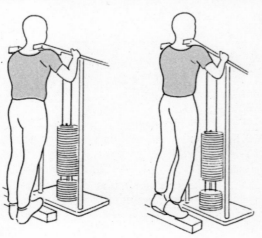

until the calf muscles are fully contracted and you have lifted yourself up on to your toes. Hold this position for the count of two and then lower your heels slowly to the initial position, taking twice as long as you took to lift up. Repeat this for your IPR.

(5) **Lunges:** Using a light to medium weighted barbell, stand with it on your shoulders as if you were squatting. From this position step forward with one foot and lower yourself slowly until the other knee touches the ground. Now, using only the muscles of the front leg, push yourself back to your starting position, once again taking twice as long as it took to gain the initial position. Next, step forward with the other leg, lowering yourself until the back knee touches the ground. Once again using only the muscles in the front leg, push yourself back to the starting position. Repeat this sequence for twenty repetitions.

(6) **Flat or inclined bench press:** For this exercise you will need the aid of a training partner. Probably the best basic chest and upper body exercise, it is an important one for all pushing–throwing–punching actions. It also stimulates growth in at least three other muscle groups – the deltoids, the trapezius and the triceps. Practised regularly, this exercise promotes good stability in the shoulder joint, the most mobile in the body and very prone to injury.

If the muscle groups around the shoulder are not strengthened this can allow too much play in the joint which can lead in some cases to dislocation. Aidan in fact experienced just such an injury, which started with a slight 'out of place' feeling after hard training sessions and led in the end to him having to undergo surgery and extensive rehabilitation to rectify the problem.

Lie back on the inclined bench and grasp the barbell with your hands approximately shoulder width apart. Lift the bar off its supports so that your arms are locked. Making sure that your elbows are kept wide, slowly lower the weight to your chest (not onto it) and hold it there for a moment, then smoothly push it back to the starting position and

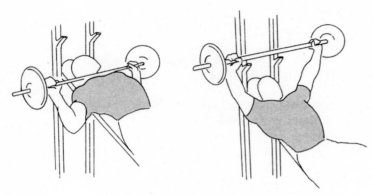

**(8) Shoulder press:** Placing a bar-bell on your shoulders as in the squats exercise, sit down on a bench. Keeping your elbows out to the sides, push the weight upwards from behind your neck until both arms are completely locked and the weight is directly overhead. Now slowly lower the bar-bell, taking twice as long as it took to raise it. Repeat this movement to your IPR and then with the assistance of your partner go for at least three to four additional forced repetitions.

repeat for your IPR. When you have reached failure point (which should be at the limit of your IPR) then your training partner can help by aiding you to lift the weight. This is not to make it easy for you; in fact these forced repetitions should be even more difficult to perform than your regular ones.

This should be continued for at least three to four repetitions. At this stage your muscle should be practically incapable of functioning at all. This is only a momentary situation, however, so do not worry. Repeat as determined in the routine. At this stage allow yourself two to three minutes to recover from the severity of the inclined bench press, before moving on to bar-bell rowing.

**(7) Bar-bell rowing:** Hold the bar-bell with your hands about shoulder width apart. Bend your knees slightly, keeping your head as high as possible, bend over so that your body is parallel to the floor, and keep your lower back flat and your buttocks pushed outwards. From this position pull up on the bar, pull it into the stomach, not the chest, and lower it slowly until your arms are completely stretched. Do not rest the weight on the floor until the set is completed. Repeat for your IPR.

**(9) Concentration curls:** Using a dumb-bell, sit down on a bench and with your left hand on your left thigh place your right elbow against the inside of your right thigh and extend your arm until the dumb-bell is close to your calf. Keeping your back as straight as possible and without jerking, curl the dumb-bell slowly up to the right side of your chest.

When the dumb-bell reaches this position hold the contraction momentarily before lowering the weight, again taking twice as long as it took to lift it. Repeat for your IPR.

When you have reached the point of positive failure, use your other hand to help lift the weight for an additional three to four forced repetitions. Now transfer the weight to your left hand and repeat the procedure for the same number of repetitions.

**(10) Triceps push down:** An excellent exercise, working all three heads of the triceps muscle. It must be performed on a lat machine. Place your hands five to six inches apart on the bar and from this position, keeping your elbows in at your sides, push the bar down towards the floor. Once your arms are completely straight, hold the contraction momentarily in your triceps and then, once more taking longer than it took to push down, allow the bar to return to the starting position. Repeat for your IPR.

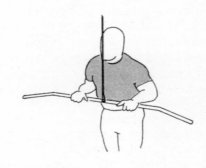

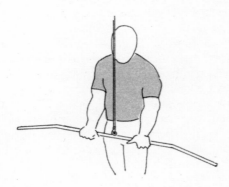

Because of the relatively light weight used in this exercise, at least at beginner and intermediate level, it is usual to have a much higher number of repetitions in each set than in the other exercises utilizing much heavier weights. Aim for at least 15 in each set for this exercise. Make sure that you do not lean your body weight into the exercise. Use only your arm muscles.

**(11) Crunches:** It is vital for the *karate-ka* to have a strong abdomen. Unfortunately most of the exercises used to strengthen the abdominal muscles are ineffective. For example, a common exercise is to hook the feet under a heavy object or a wall bar and with the legs bent carry out a 'sit-up' for a number of repetitions. This is ineffective because the hip is not bent enough to disengage the iliopsoas muscle, and because the feet are supported the body is able to sit up without great effort at all on the part of the abdominal muscles.

The same applies to those perennial gym favourites, slant-board sit-ups, straight leg raises, and Roman chair sit-ups. These exercises also work primarily the illiopsoas muscles which originate in the lower back, come across the top of the pelvis and join at the thighs. Whenever these particular muscles are brought into play the abdominals assume a secondary role of fixing and stabilizing the trunk. Of course your abdominals do get tired, but they are not being exercised effectively.

A far better way to exercise the abdominals is to make sure that your feet are unsupported and your hips strongly flexed. Try, for example, lying on your back with your buttocks close to a wall and your feet placed flat on the wall, your knees bent. From this position, with your hands on your ears, sit up until your head touches your knees. From this posture it is possible to do only half a sit-up, but that will give maximum contraction of the abdominal muscles without bending the hips.

Another different abdominal muscle training exercise is given here, where the trunk is twisted as the body is raised.

The main point to remember in all abdominal exercises is to make sure that the movement takes place at your spine before any movement takes place at the hip joint. Try to maintain a sensation of curling up the spine one vertebra at a time, and when in the raised position try to give one more squeeze. Repeat the selected crunch as directed in the routine.

If you continue these exercises over the suggested period of time, there is no doubt that you will find that your overall strength will have increased, allowing you to execute your karate techniques with greater power and to sustain effort over a longer period. You will also find that your increased body strength will enable you to absorb a blow more easily than before.

# Chapter 8 **THE USE OF EQUIPMENT**

Auxiliary equipment has always had its place in the practice of karate. Initially it was constructed from readily available material: stone, rope, bamboo, iron – all were called into service to construct training aids which would help the *karate-ka* to develop the power of his blocking and striking techniques.

Probably the best-known example would be the *makiwara* or striking post, used to temper and harden the parts of the body used in striking. Although seemingly out of favour currently, and to an extent superseded by the bag and mitt, Vince and I feel that – used judiciously – there is still room for the *makiwara* in the *dojo*.

Using the *makiwara* ensures that you make a good fist and that you keep the wrist strong. It also conditions the knuckles so that strong blows can be delivered without causing self-injury. It is more effective than pad or bag in the developing of strong

*An early photo of Kanazawa Sensei in the first Nottingham dojo shortly after the introduction of karate into Great Britain*

knuckles. Do not make the supporting post too rigid, however, as the *makiwara* must give with the technique, allowing the fist or foot to penetrate the target, not simply bounce off. Too hard and the hips cannot be put into the technique properly, and the joints can be harmed by too much jarring.

The makiwara is a 'cheap and cheerful' piece of training equipment, easily made and easily repaired, not taking up much storage space. This is important when you consider that many *dojo* are used for other purposes as well, cannot afford expensive equipment, and have no real storage space for large items.

Having said that, we would advise all *karate-ka* to devote regular periods to training with equipment, particularly as much is now available in an affordable price range, and frankly without it you will never develop the full potential of your blows.

In Nottingham I coach the county squad made up of fighters from all different styles and associations, and when practising with air shields I am continually reminded of the difference that bag and pad training makes, as those unused to it contact with bad technique, sometimes falling short of the target, sometimes getting too close, and frequently hurting themselves by not keeping the wrist strong. Kicking techniques either bounce off the shield, or, what is worse, miss altogether!

Of all the equipment now available we feel that at the very least everyone should practise with the kick and punch bag for power of leg and arm strikes, and focus mitts to develop speed and timing. There is now on the market a type of bag with an impact-measuring device attached, which can be used in a variety of ways to measure and enhance the speed and power of blows. One point to remember is that any sustained period of heavy bag work tends to slow down the delivery of techniques, as the attention is on building up the power. To prevent this make sure that you follow such a period with some light fast techniques into the air to reinforce the body's 'memory' of the correct speed of execution.

## The bag

The bag should be filled with tightly packed scraps of leather or rags, never (at least to begin with) with sand or sawdust, as these compact down with use into a concrete-like lump, and can damage the fist or foot. Avoid the temptation to make it too heavy until you have mastered the technique, at which time you can increase the weight.

*Vince and Aidan during a workout on the heavy bag*

*Aidan and Vince: combination practice with focus mitts*

When using the bag to practise kicks it is useful to swing it away from you first, so that you also get the timing and distance practice as it swings back towards you. Doing this will also enable you to get the feel of an opponent's weight coming on to you, and to practise your stopping kicks.

Using air shields or arm-held kick bags is an excellent way to help students practise sinking the hips into the technique. The bag should be held close to the body and the person holding it moves around, offering the kicker a realistic moving target. This helps to remedy some basic faults, such as that seen in basic front kick where the foot just glances off the target in an upwards arc because the hips are held too far back. The ability to feel the kick penetrate the target develops the power of the kick much faster than simply performing the technique into the air.

## Focus mitts

These are very good for developing speed, focus and power in both hand and foot techniques, as well as improving the ability to hit a specific target. Try if you can to work with two mitts, as this will enable you to practise a greater variety of combination punching, or combinations of hand and foot techniques.

Although practice with focus mitts is carried out initially statically, with one partner holding them still in position for the kick, punch or strike, they are extremely good for developing hand and eye coordination and footwork. To practice this the partner wearing the mitts begins by standing still and moving them slowly in circular motions, to give practice in hitting a moving target. As skill and co-ordination increase, the pads can be moved more quickly and the holder can begin to move around the *dojo*, briefly offering targets and then removing them. This helps to give the attacker practice in aiming at a ducking or weaving target, and improves anticipation.

One step on from this is for the wearer to show a target and, if the striker does not maintain a good guard or safe distance, hit him with one of the pads. This will force the attacker to maintain his or her concentration at all times. Do try to make sure that you return to a good strong and balanced stance after throwing your technique.

Remember that when you make use of any of this sort of equipment you must concentrate on developing a specific aspect of your technique. Do not just get out the bag or pads and spend time simply whacking at them. Decide in advance what you need to concentrate on and devote the time only to that. Most important of all, you must concentrate and keep a sense of reality about your practice. Treat the bag, pad, air-shield, *makiwara* or mitt as your opponent and therefore with respect and your complete attention.

# Chapter 9 COMPETITION (SPORT) KARATE

Mitsusuke Harada, head of Shoto-kai Karate-dō in Great Britain, confirms in conversation that there was a disagreement over the way in which karate was developing between Funakoshi Gichin, who wished to retain the emphasis on *kate*, and his son Yoshitaka, who believed in a more pragmatic type of karate. Ever since free-sparring was introduced into the practice of karate in the 1930s this conflict has continued to be unresolved, and there have been arguments between traditionalists, who decry competition karate as dancing, light ineffectual technique, cultivation of the ego, etc., and the sport-orientated *karate-ka* who maintains that as fighting and competition are the primary objectives, then the practice of basics and *kata* are simply a waste of time, it being far better to start free-practice (*ju-kumite*) as soon as possible.

In our opinion both views are narrow and incorrect. Aidan and I would go so far as to say to the traditionalist that every student should at some time or other take part in competition. It can sometimes be the case that an uncertain *karate-ka* can shy away from competition by claiming that competition goes against the principles of karate-dō. Frankly, this is rubbish! What would this student say to the argument that competition allows one of the only opportunities (other than street fighting) to test skill of technique and, more importantly perhaps, composure (*zanshin*)? Surely what is important is not the fact that you compete, but the reason why you compete.

Masatoshi Nakayama, late head of the Japanese Karate Association (in an article in Terry O'Neill's excellent *Fighting Arts* magazine, vol. 6, No. 1,) commenting on the fact that no matches were held in Okinawa and that the training was essentially *kata* based, states:

Although we can maintain our technique through practice without an opponent, we cannot improve our mental and physical conditioning in preparation for actual battle. Specifically we need to learn how to overcome anxiety or how far we should stand from an opponent. Without practice against an opponent we cannot have the chance to work at our greatest capacity.

In the end Nakayama's solution to the quandary was to institute the first all-Japan grand karate tournament in October 1957, which comprised free-style fighting and *kata*. And yes, competition karate does have rules against the use of dangerous techniques;

this is why *kata* and *yakusoku kumite* (prearranged sparring) are practised in the *dojo*.

Conversely the student who is interested only in competition success should bear in mind that by its very nature, being a good competitor does not mean that one is automatically a good *karate-ka*. Indeed, too much emphasis on this element, to the detriment of the other aspects, can lead to a false conception of one's ability. It should not be lightly dismissed that most of the acknowledged world masters in karate-dō have been *kata* winners as well as *kumite* champions.

Over the last ten years or so competition karate has changed dramatically. From the basically static one-point match we have moved to the system of three full points or six half points to decide the winner, allowing and encouraging a faster and freer exchange of techniques over a longer period. This, combined with the far greater number of events open to a competitor today, has led to the emergence of a different kind of competitor. Physically he or she is younger and more athletic, and mentally better adapted to the pressures of competition.

This vast increase in the number of competitions and the importance now placed upon them has led to the emergence of some hitherto unexpected problems which are inherent in karate, and in competition karate in particular. Traditionally the Western *karate-ka* have looked to the senior Japanese instructors as their role models. Unfortunately some of these *budo* masters, these combinations of physical power tempered with compassion, humility and learning, resulting from a lifetime's arduous training and discipline, have been seen to have feet of clay.

Senior students, because of their very closeness to their *sensei*, often gain insights denied the average *karate-ka*. Competitors at world-class events have fallen victim to bias and serious failures in etiquette and honour, often perpetrated by very senior figures from whom a better example was to be expected. We have seen over the years numerous examples of senior experienced and very good (but non-Japanese) referees being arbitrarily pushed aside to make room for a senior Japanese figurehead who would appear to make up the rules as he went along. Even at world level there is video evidence of refereeing which, at the kindest, can only be called totally incompetent and inept, but which has led to a world title being wrongly awarded.

*Opposite: Aidan demonstrates his superb kicking ability*

Lack of respect and incompetence or bias are not necessarily features of the younger instructor, but can also be found in respected figures of many years' standing. Recognizing that this is so imposes even greater demands upon the mental toughness of a *karate-ka*. He must learn that, unlike in the West, the Japanese demand respect as a right, not as something to be earned. He must learn that in some cases respect and humility are essentially one-way traffic, from him to his *sensei*. It is sometimes a personal revelation to realize that *sensei* is still a man and can have a mere mortal's faults. This must lead to a resetting of personal goals; now not to emulate, but to surpass.

Unfortunately, although these difficulties can be resolved in one's personal training, it is not so easy for the top-level competitor who should have the absolute right to expect a fair, honest and unbiased appraisal of his or her efforts. It is one thing to lose to an opponent's superior techniques, or to one's own lapse of attention; it is something else entirely to lose to a bad decision.

Thankfully, in the major inter-style events these problems with bias have been largely resolved, but they still tend to prevail in some single-style or Association events. The referee's duty is extremely demanding and arduous; he must strive to demonstrate the depths of his *budo* by his obvious and scrupulous fairness and integrity. Failing this, the competitor is forced to accept that, as in many other areas, life is unfair and bad decisions do occur.

What is important here is that the competitive athlete follows the advice given in the section dealing with mental preparation, and sets goals for which he is totally and fully responsible, where success or failure is not measured by the winning of the trophy, but by the achieving of the goals.

In this chapter we hope to show some of the many techniques that have evolved over the years, as well as some of the 'dos and don'ts' that will help you to use them successfully. It will help if you try to remember these important factors: timing, distance, agility, flexibility, speed, explosive power, reaction time, mental awareness and above all courage and controlled aggression. You may not excel in all of these, but you should aim to reach a reasonable standard in them all.

One of the main faults which becomes apparent in some *karate-ka* who specialize in competition-orientated karate is a bias towards one favourite technique. Although many of our greatest fighters are well known for a particular technique, to reach the top and stay there takes a strong and varied repertoire. If, for example, you are good at a particular kicking technique, you may start out by scoring with it consistently. Nevertheless, after a few competitions somebody will work it out, and that's all it takes – so don't be predictable.

The rules of competition which predominate

*Aidan scoring on Dagfelt (Sw.), Madrid*

today encourage a more mobile style of fighting, with the opportunity to go for more spectacular techniques. This being so, it is important to confuse your opponents, 'mess them about' so to speak. You should continually change the distance between you and your opponent, change stance, feint with punches and lift the knee as if to kick in order to test your opponent's reaction. You should aim to dominate and control your opponent by finding his weaknesses. Does he stand his ground when under pressure, or does he back away and become a more defensive fighter? Is he impetuously aggressive, charging in at the slightest hint of opportunity?

When you have this information then you choose your strategy and the techniques that are available to you, and of course, at all times be aware that your opponent could (and should) be doing exactly the same thing. This may seem a long process, but it should take up no more than the first 30 seconds or so of the bout.

Although somewhat simplistic, it is convenient to categorize your opponents into two types: the kicker and the puncher.

# The kicker

The kicker will usually feint with his hands to make his opponent move slightly back, making him feel that he is a safe distance away, whereas in fact the kicker has put his opponent at just the right distance to enable him to use his legs.

It is important for a kicker to remember to keep his guard up in case his kick is blocked and he has left no defence against his opponent's counter punch. It is also important that the knee of the attacking leg must be high, even if it is a middle-range (*chudan*) kick. The high knee serves as a guard, because the kicker is at his most vulnerable when he is half-way through his technique. If the knee is kept high, as shown in the illustrations, there should be no target for the counter punch.

Kicks can be used not only as attacking techniques, but also as defensive ones. When defending with kicks you can use several methods. For instance, if you have finished reverse punch (*gyaku-zuki*) and it has been blocked, then as you pull back with your weight on your back leg your front leg can deliver a roundhouse kick (*mawashi-geri*) or back roundhouse kick (*ushiro-mawashi-geri*). This technique has been used successfully by

*H. Ochi showing a classic* mawashi-geri

many fighters. (Actually Vince learned this the hard way in a bout for the Shotokan Karate International final placings when he was caught with just this technique from seemingly impossible close range.)

Another technique is to draw your opponent into making a rash attack by giving him an open target or by taunting or intimidating him. Then, when he attacks, and just as his feet come together, you thrust your front side kick (*yoko-geri kekomi*) into his mid-section. This technique usually results in your opponent being floored, but if this is not the case then at least it will stop him dead in his tracks!

# The puncher

Although punching techniques tend to take less skill than kicking, it takes a lot more courage to use them, as it is necessary to get close in to your opponent and that makes you vulnerable. As a puncher it is especially necessary for you to move in against a kicker so that you close the distance and cancel

*Jeoff Thompson, WUKO world heavyweight champion, one of the world's best punchers*

the kicks out. The reverse punch is probably the most widely used technique in karate, and not far behind in popularity is the backfist strike (*uraken*), both hand techniques.

However, many of the principles that were mentioned in the kicking section can also be used for the puncher – drawing out your opponent's attack for example. You can draw out a counter punch by jutting the hips forward and giving the opponent a target that he – because of his reaction training – finds impossible to resist. Then, as he counter punches, you pull your hips back, blocking his counter and delivering your own attack.

When attacking, double and triple combination punches are very useful and can be used when trying to force an opponent out of the area. If your opponent has been warned for leaving the competition area to escape your attacks and is in danger of losing a point (*jogai*), you can often force him out with this technique.

One important point, especially with your punching techniques, is the proper extension of the technique. Some fighters tend to keep the shoulder and hips too far back as this is how they have been taught in basics, but this can cost you as much as a foot in distance – extra penetration which would enable you to score on your opponent. Also, to gain distance and penetration the front leg must be extended, even though you may feel vulnerable to sweeps by being extended to this degree. Obviously to some extent this is true, but the advantages far outweigh the disadvantages.

# Sweeping techniques

With a few notable exceptions, sweeping and hooking techniques have been greatly neglected over the past few years, which is a great pity as the effect of a successful sweep is obvious. While you are standing up, your opponent is flat on his back or face, whichever the case may be. A totally demoralizing position to end up in. I think that one of the main reasons for this neglect lies in the *dojo*

training for these techniques, because in order to master sweeps and hooks you have to take quite a few knocks in practice. The bruises, knocks and sprains that your legs and feet suffer can be off-putting in the early stages.

The key to sweeping is to exploit the weaknesses of your opponent's stance. This may involve a direct sweep attack, where you may have to draw

*Roy Harrison shows a perfect double foot sweep*

your opponent out and weaken his position, forcing him on to one leg, or even take him down while he is delivering a kick himself.

One very important principle of the sweep, probably the most important, is to keep your body weight low; your centre of gravity must be as low as possible, and to do this you must keep your supporting leg bent. Another vital principle is to keep your guard at all times. As with many of the other techniques that are covered, if the technique does not work you must be prepared to block and counter.

One common fault is that when going for the sweep, as your opponent lifts his leg, the momentum of your leg spins your body round, leaving you with your back exposed to your opponent – with obvious repercussions. The way to counteract this is to thrust your opposite hand forward, rotating your upper body in the opposite direction to the spin.

You must also be aware of the position in which your opponent will fall – forward on his face, backward away from you or wherever. Knowing this will enable you to drop into your stance accordingly, and deliver the finishing blow as cleanly and as quickly as possible. It is important to remember that a sweep in itself will not score a point; the finishing technique is most important.

In conclusion, it is important that you practice a technique constantly in the *dojo*, repeating it over and over again before using it in competition. Through doing this you not only become acquainted with the technique mentally, but your body learns the movements of the technique and, therefore, it becomes second nature to you, because with all the pressures that are on you in competition you need to have the confidence to use the technique effectively.

Always keep your competition training realistic – too much relaxed free style can give you a false sense of distance. Keep the partner work intensive and your awareness constant. Aidan and I refer to this as keeping a sense of danger in your techniques. Learn to 'read' your opponent before you engage; the acquisition of this skill, as with all the others, lies in correct training and in experience.

# Main competition techniques

## Gyaku zuki (reverse punch)

It is appropriate that I begin with this technique as it is the most widely used in karate competition. It is usually used with a feint when attacking, but is probably most effective as a counter punch by blocking, 'digging in' strongly into your stance and using the power in your hips to drive the punch in. This use of the hips makes the reverse punch a particularly powerful and effective counter.

When attacking with this punch one important point, as mentioned before, is the extension of the front foot. Too much and it will leave your stance weak, too short and you won't catch your opponent, leaving you open for a counter. Sliding forward or thrusting the hips forward must be employed when attacking.

**Some common faults when using this technique**

(1) **Narrow stance:** Using too narrow a stance. If the stance is too narrow this restricts your hip movement and also the stability of the stance. If the hip is too far back and not square, then you have no power in the punch, especially when using it defensively with your opponent's body weight coming towards you. If your hips are not square at the moment of impact your counter will lack power and you can be overwhelmed and pushed out of the area.

(2) **Hesitation:** He who hesitates is lost. Some fighters tend to think too much before firing punches, a *gyaku zuki* punch especially, as it is a very fast technique. If you see an opening then just let the technique fly.

(3) **Lack of extension of the front leg:** When punching, if the front leg is not far enough advanced, and you have the knee deeply bent and you lean your weight forward over the front leg, it is very difficult for you to come back again. You must stretch forward with the front leg, win the point and be in a position to pull your body back by thrusting off the front leg.

## Mawashi geri (roundhouse kick)

This kick is a very popular one and it can be very spectacular. There is generally no doubt about scoring when this technique lands, especially to the head. Used mostly as an attacking kick, it can also be used defensively.

The key to this kick is the high knee lift. The high knee is most important and serves as a guard against any counter punch when the kicker is at his most vulnerable half-way through his technique. Lifting the knee high also allows you to disguise the actual technique until the last moment, as from this initial position you can throw a straightforward roundhouse kick, a side thrust kick, a back roundhouse kick, or indeed, a combination of kicks, which can further serve to confuse your opponent.

In competition you don't have the time to have a large wind-up technique in this kick, kicking in classical style in a large circular motion, with the knee going out to the side, as it leaves you too open to counter attacks, and it takes too long. Therefore, the power must come from the knee rather than the hip.

**Some common faults when using this technique**

(1) **Not maintaining defence:** Dropping the guard when attacking. As mentioned earlier, the kicker is at his most vulnerable at the mid-point of this technique, with the feet coming together about to lift the leg. At this point you must keep your arms in a good guard position and don't leave it too late before lifting the knee – and remember to keep it high.

(2) **Not using full-range hip movement:** Keeping the hip back when delivering the kick. This is a common fault, for when we learn this kick we are taught to twist the upper body in the opposite direction to the direction of the leg in order to counteract the momentum of the foot travelling in a large arc.

This is fine when the kick is used at close distance, but when it is at long range you need extension.

Also the chest becomes a large target when you kick in this manner, and you tend to be very close to your opponent which means that your supporting leg can be easily swept.

## Mae geri (front kick)

*Mae-geri* is a very strong and effective technique, although it is one that does not seem to be used as often in competition now as it once was. One reason for this is that it tends to be a '*kamikaze*' or 'suicide' technique, as it is very difficult to pull the body back after it has been extended and the hips thrust forward.

In basic practice students spend a lot of time practising a snap *mae-geri*, where the hips are sharply thrust forward and immediately snapped back again, with the body falling back into the original stance. In fact, practically all *mae-geri* scored in competition are thrust kicks, which lead you into moving forward, and because the hips are mostly square to the front this gives your opponent a large target.

Another problem that can occur with *mae geri* is that unless your kicks are accurate you run the risk of crunching your toes on the opponent's knee. This can serve as a great discouragement in the early stages when learning this kick.

*Bill Wallace ('Superfoot') stresses the importance of the high knee position*

## Some important points when using this technique

(1) Keep your guard at all times. If your kick is blocked you must be in a position to block and counter attack.
(2) Lift the knee high. This is very important if you want to avoid injuries to the toes by connecting with your opponent's knee.
(3) Use feints. This will clear the way for the delivery of the kick and make the impact more effective.

## Yoko-geri (side kick)

The side kick is a power technique rarely used to good effect. One reason for this is that it should be used with a feint when used as an attacking technique, and when used defensively your distance and centre of gravity play an important part.

As with all kicks, the high knee position is vitally important. It is identical to that in *mawashi-geri* and reverse *mawashi-geri*, thus making it difficult for your opponent to identify the kick until it is too late.

The correct use of the hips and body weight is also essential, especially when bringing your opponent on to the kick, i.e. drawing his attack.

## Some important points when using this technique

(1) When attacking, keep the body low so that the distance between you and your opponent is covered. Don't jump in an upward arc as is often seen. This tends to telegraph the technique to your opponent and enables him to block or evade the kick.
(2) When drawing your opponent on to your kick you must allow for his bodyweight coming forward, therefore your own centre of gravity must be well forward and your timing spot on. You must catch your opponent with the feet together, before his technique is fully committed, as this is the weakest point in the attack.
(3) Use a feint when attacking. This is also very important as the opponent's guard must be lifted in order to expose the mid-section and to ensure that your kick has the greatest effect.

*Aidan in action: superb extension in the side thrust kick*

### Ushiro-mawashi-geri (reverse roundhouse kick)

This is not an easy kick to master by any means. It is, however, a kick that has been used a lot more over recent years with great effect. If used correctly this technique can catch an opponent dead. It can be very effective when hooked around a block, and even if the opponent moves in towards you the hooking action of the leg enables you to hit him on the back of the head (although being this close is not desirable, as you can be overwhelmed and swept).

This kick can be used off the front foot or the back, using feints. Some fighters use the kick as they counter, hooking it around high as the opponent attacks. Again, a high knee position is of the utmost importance.

### Some important points when using this technique

(1) The line of attack. This is important in many different techniques but especially so with this kick, as the danger of being swept is always present. You should, if possible, attack your opponent from an opposite stance, i.e. if you are kicking off the front foot in right stance your opponent will be in left stance. Not only is it easier for you to hook around a block from this opposite stance, but it is more difficult for your opponent to lean back away from the kick as his spine restricts his backward movement.

(2) Ensure that your kick is not deflected. If your opponent deflects your kick you could land with your back to your opponent and therefore open

*Aidan again: a reverse roundhouse finds its mark*

to a full point score against you. One way of avoiding this is to ensure that your feint takes your opponent's guard or block in the opposite direction, therefore leaving the target clear for your kick.

# AIDAN

Left to right: Jeoff Thompson, Pat McKay, Ticky Donovan and Aidan (Madrid 1983)

Recognition of World Championship success

Receiving trophy from Hirokasu Kanazawa

Going for the Kill! England v. USA

A lighter moment. Training with Shukokai fighters G. Cross and K. Johnson

T. Donovan, Aidan and Dominique Valera

# VINCE

The infamous Kisami-zuki

Sparring with Kobarra

Receiving medal from Asano Sensei

The SKI European squad

SKI Team Champions, 1977

After training with JKA instructor Sode

# Chapter 10 **COMPETITION COMBINATIONS**

Note that when feint techniques are described in the following text it must be understood that these should be believable, sharp and strong techniques, sometimes delivered short of the target and sometimes not executed to completion. In all cases they will be effective only if your opponent believes in them. In some instances it will help to do the technique properly first to instil a sense of expectation in your opponent.

## (1) **Stance left to left.**

The attacker, keeping his body well back, feints a kick to his opponent's shin to draw his attention downwards. Immediately a second feint kick is snapped to the mid-section, and without withdrawing the leg the final and main attack is made with a strong kick to the head. The idea is to execute all three kicks in rapid succession; the first two are feints, but must be strong enough to be believable.

## (2) Stance left to right.

The attacker feints with a snap punch to the head and immediately follows up with a reverse punch, again to the head. Keeping this second punch out with the fist close to the opponent's face will cause him to keep his guard up and his attention on the fist. This will give an opportunity for the attacker to slide in and hit to the mid-section with a roundhouse kick.

## (3) Stance left to left.

This is a fairly simple but effective combination. You trick your opponent into anticipating a front kick by lifting your knee high, as in the first stage of a front kick. This will force him to begin to react by preparing to block a kick to the front of his body. At this stage, keeping the knee high, thrust your hips forward and change to a roundhouse kick to the head. If done correctly your leg will travel over the top of his block.

## (4) **Stance left to left.**

In a continual sequence the attacker feints with a leading hand snap punch to the head, then a reverse punch to the body followed by a second snap punch or open hand strike to the head. Leave the last punch extended to cover your opponent's vision, and follow with a strong roundhouse kick to the head. The speed of this combination, plus the up and down nature of the attacks, serves to confuse the opponent.

## (5) **Stance left to left.**

In a large exaggerated motion, the attacker swings his arm over his head towards the opponent, forcing him to raise his guard. At the same time he executes a front kick with the rear leg to the opponent's mid-section. The punch and kick make contact at the same time.

## (6) **Stance left to left.**

The attacker swings his arm in an exaggerated circular motion towards the opponent, and then back overhead. At the same time the front knee is lifted and the body slides forward. The knee lift is turned into a roundhouse kick to the head. The idea is to draw the opponent's attention to the exaggerated arm action, and thus away from the kick. It is important that as the arm goes back the body slides in, and the kick should be timed to contact when the arm reaches its furthest point to the rear.

## (7) Stance left to left.

The attacker juts his hips momentarily forward, giving the opponent an obvious but fleeting target (leaving the hips forward too long makes the ploy too obvious!). As the opponent attacks with reverse punch, sharply pull in your hips and front leg into cat stance (*neko-ashi-dachi*), pushing the punch downward with one hand and at the same time delivering a punch to the head with the other. It is important to pull your groin well back or you will simply redirect your opponent's punch to this area.

## (8) **Stance right to left.**

As your opponent attacks with *gyaku-zuki*, you move in with your front leg and while twisting your body out of the line of the punch you wrap your rear arm over the punching arm and sweep away his front leg with the back of your own leg. Finish with a punch while controlling the opponent's prone body and maintaining a tight grip on his arm.

## (9) **Stance left to left.**

Sharply raise your front hand as a feint to lift the opponent's guard, and at the same time lift your front knee high and slide forward to deliver a middle-level roundhouse kick. It is important to slide in, not heel step (i.e. bringing the back foot to the front foot before pushing forward) – this takes too long and also warns the opponent that you are coming.

b

c

## (10) **Stance left to left.**

Lean forward and attack with snap punch to the head to lift the opponent's guard. As his hands lift spin and attack with middle level back kick.

Vince has had much success with a variation of this technique, beginning with a fast fake backfist strike instead of a snap punch. In this variation make sure that you do not fully complete the first feint attack; jerk the elbow sharply at the opponent, and spin immediately he reacts.

a

c

b

d

## (11) **Stance right to left.**

Attack with reverse punch to middle level to lower the opponent's guard. As he blocks bring the back foot up and attack with snap punch to the head. Leave this punch extended to obscure your opponent's vision, and finish with back roundhouse kick to the head. The obscuring hand will cover the lift of your knee prior to the kick.

## (12) **Stance right to left.**

Slide forward and lift your front knee high to give the impression that you are going to attack with back roundhouse kick. As your opponent's guard lifts thrust your hips forward and execute middle-level side thrust kick. As you lift your knee hesitate briefly to see the opponent's reaction. If the guard does not lift then you can attack with roundhouse kick or back roundhouse kick from the same knee position.

## (13) **Stance left to left.**

Feint an attack with reverse punch, then raise your stance and disguise this with a second feint punch to the head with your leading hand. As his stance and guard lift, jump into the air and spin, delivering a back kick to the opponent's mid-section while still in the air.

## (14) **Stance right to left.**

This technique must be carried out in one flowing, continuous movement. Feint a front hand snap punch to the head, immediately followed by a reverse punch to the head. This should take your opponent's guard across his body and disguise your leg movements. As you execute the second punch you simultaneously attack with heel kick (*kakato-geri* – sometimes called 'axe kick') to the head.

A variation of this is to attack as before with the hand techniques but instead of the heel kick execute a crescent kick (*mikazuki-geri*) over your opponent's head without making contact, and, as your leg drops, sweep away his front leg causing him to fall on to his face. Finish with a kick to the mid-section.

## (15) Stance right to left.

This technique is best used when your opponent is in a high stance. You can often make him assume a shorter higher stance by continually attacking with sweeps. Slide forward, bringing your back leg behind and past your front leg. Disguise this by feinting a punch to the head with your front hand in order to raise his guard. Immediately lifting the front leg high in front of your opponent, jump to place your other leg behind him and in a scissor-like motion take him down and finish with a heel kick.

## (16) **Stance left to left.**

Leaving an opening, you entice your opponent into attacking with a front kick. Pull your front leg back, twist the body away from the line of the kick and block with the left forearm. Block strongly so as to disturb his balance and with a hooking type action, force him into a longer stance. Immediately spin and deliver back roundhouse kick to the head.

## (17) **Stance left to left.**

A variation of the above, again use your blocking action to make sure that your opponent lengthens his stance. As his kicking leg is still in the air drop down low, sweeping your rear leg round in a circle to chop away his kicking leg as it lands.

## (18) **Stance right to left.**

Entice your opponent into attacking with front hand snap punch. As he does, pull back your front leg while parrying the punch with your front shoulder and covering the fist with your rear hand. At the same time, lift your front knee high and deliver a back roundhouse kick to the head. As your leg retracts, bring it down in a sweeping motion against the inside of your opponent's front leg. Your front hand pushes his shoulder to his front. This will cause him to fall forwards on to his face whereupon you can finish with a kick.

*An early competition photo of Vince in action, powering an opponent off his feet*

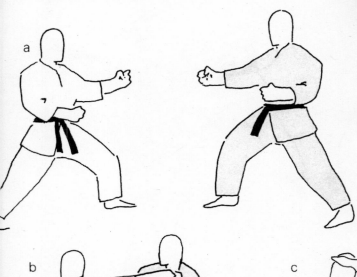

## (19) **Stance left to left.**

Attack strongly with a front hand snap punch in a rolling motion somewhat to the inside of your opponent's face, causing him to overblock to the inside. Keep the circular movement going and with the elbow high attack to the outside of his head with backfist. Finish with middle level reverse punch. You should make sure that when executing the rolling, feinting motion it is done so quickly that your opponent's block does not make contact. This will ensure that he will overblock and leave a target for your main attack.

## (20) Stance right to left or left to left.

As your opponent attacks with a lunge punch or reverse punch, twist your body and jump high into the air, blocking with your rear hand while punching strongly to his head or chest with the other. Jump as high as you can and keep the twist going so that you land at a 45-degree angle to the line of his attack in a position to follow up with another kick or punch.

## (21) **Stance right to left.**

Attack with a reverse punch and immediately follow by sliding the rear leg in, lifting the front knee high and delivering a roundhouse kick to the head. The opponent blocks but you maintain the high knee position and as his guard begins to drop you kick again. The kicks should be in rapid succession, and you can even deliver three if necessary.

## (22) **Stance left to left.**

The idea of this combination is to draw out the opponent's reverse punch. Feint a front kick to the mid-section, keeping your hips well back so that his counter does not catch you. You virtually fall backwards, turning as you block his punch, and straight away deliver a back kick to his now unprotected mid-section.

## (23) **Stance left to left.**

Attack with a middle-level front kick, landing with your foot outside your opponent's front foot. Make sure that you kick to the outside of his body, forcing him to block with downward block (*gedan barai*).
As you are bringing your kicking leg down, block his counterpunch with your own downward block and simultaneously strike to the head with backfist. Sweep his front leg with your kicking leg, while grabbing his shoulder with your front hand and forcing him in the opposite direction. Finish with a heel kick.

## (24) Stance right to right.

Attack with a middle-level reverse punch, at the same time thrusting the other hand over the shoulder of the punching arm with the elbow held high. Attack with backfist strike to the head, at the same time bringing the feet together, and stepping forward execute reverse punch as before. The type of footwork here is that called 'following foot' (*tsugi-ashi*) where the same foot is kept forward, the rear foot coming up to join it and then thrusting it forward again.

A variation of this is to attack with the reverse punch and backfist strike as before, forcing your opponent to block the backfist. Stepping up as before, this time execute a front foot roundhouse kick to the head.

## (25) **Stance left to left.**

Attack with a snap punch to the head, leaving your mid-section open, anticipating your opponent's reverse punch counter. In a recoil action twist your body out of the line of his counter, bringing your back foot round and at the same time pulling the punching hand back and down to block the counter. Straight away punch to the head again with the same hand and finish with a reverse punch. It is important to shift your body so that you are at an angle to your opponent.

## (26) Stance right to left.

Stand in opposite stance to your opponent, with your hips square on so as to offer a big target to entice him into attacking with a front kick. As the kick comes, do not attempt to block it; move straight in with your front leg at the same time twisting your hips so that the kick brushes past your body. Grab his kicking leg with your rear hand while thrusting your front hand around his waist. You then spin round with your back foot going behind you, and now you are both facing in the same direction. Clasping him tightly to you, sweep your other leg against his supporting leg. As he lands keep his legs apart and finish with a punch to the body. The faster the kick the easier this technique is, as you use your opponent's strength and weight against him. Move in to cancel the kick and sweep him, keeping close so that you become the centre of a circle with him on the outside.

*Aidan showing combination no. 26 in competition*

You can also perform this technique when in left to
left stance. This will cause the opponent to land
on his face rather than on his back.

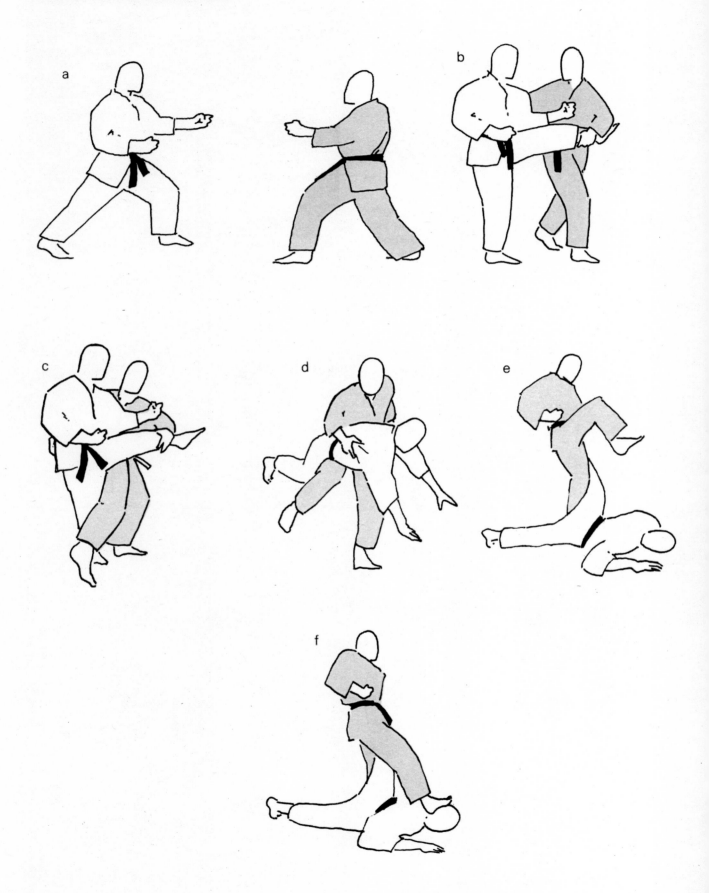

## (27) Stance left to left.

Attack by jutting your hips forward to draw out your opponent's counter punch. As he punches pull the hips back and deflect his punch with your rear hand. Keeping the front hand high, thrust your front leg deeply in towards the opponent, pushing his punching hand strongly away with your front arm, and then deliver a strong reverse punch to his mid-section. This combination should be done in one flowing movement which adds great power to the final punch.

## (28) Stance left to left.

As your opponent attacks with a roundhouse kick to the head, move in and to his inside with a pressing block to his shin with your front hand, while simultaneously sweeping his supporting leg before he can retract the kick and regain stability. Finish with a punch to the body.

## (29) Stance left to left.

Entice your opponent into attacking with a front kick. Pull your front leg back and at the same time hook the kicking leg upwards with your front arm. As his leg is still in the air, spin your back leg around, sweeping his supporting leg away, and finish with a reverse punch or heel kick. It is important to keep your hips low when executing the sweep.

## (30) **Stance right to right.**

With your back leg, sweep your opponent's front leg (*ashi-barai*). Do this hard a number of times and he will begin to anticipate this technique and lift his front leg. As he does this, in one flowing movement continue the sweep and step through, spinning and bringing your back leg around to sweep his supporting leg away. Finish with reverse punch or heel kick.

## (31) **Stance left to left.**

Attack as before with a foot sweep to your
opponent's front leg but as soon as you make contact
and he begins to shift his balance pull the attacking
foot back, lift the knee and thrust your hips
forwards delivering a middle-level front kick.
Remember to keep your guard up at all times.

## (32) **Stance left to left.**

Slide forward and attack with a low mid-level reverse punch to make your opponent drop his guard to cover it. As his hand goes down, bring up the back foot, pull back the punching hand, lift the elbow high and stepping forward deliver a backfist strike to his head. Finish with a middle-level reverse punch.

NB: This combination must be done in one fast sequence, with the first punch arcing downwards making the opponent overblock. The rolling motion continues up into the backfist strike. This continuous movement gives him nothing to make contact with, and by the time he has brought his hand back up to try to stop the backfist he is too late.

*Aidan, England v. USA, Crystal Palace*

## (33) **Stance left to left.**

Begin by attacking with a high reverse punch to lift your opponent's guard. As his hand lifts, execute a mid-level roundhouse kick to his kidney area with your rear leg.

## (34) Stance left to left.

Attack by lifting the knee high and with a thrusting motion of the hips deliver a roundhouse kick to the opponent's kidney area. Keeping the body low and well back, drop the kicking leg outside the opponent's front foot and sweep it away. Finish with heel kick.

## (35) Stance left to left.

Attack with a reverse punch to your opponent's mid-section, bringing his guard down. As he begins to block your first punch, bring your back foot up and simultaneously deliver a snap punch to his head with your front hand. Thrusting your front leg strongly forward, attack again with middle-level reverse punch.

The idea of this up and down combination is to force your opponent to attempt to block all the punches, moving from high block to low block, thus leaving gaps in his guard. Because he is not expecting three punches, his own counter-punching fist will tend to remain cocked on his hip as he tries to block all the techniques with his front hand while waiting for an opportunity to catch you with his counter punch. The speed of the combination and the thrusting forward motion of the attacker makes it impossible for him to block all the punches.

(Jeoff Thompson virtually won the WUKO World Heavyweight title with this combination.)

*A strobe camera captures the sequence*

a

b

c

d

## (36) **Stance left to left.**

Start your attack by delivering a fast, strong front hand punch to the head, forcing your opponent to block hard. This will set up an expectation in his mind which will make him block in the same forceful manner when he sees what he thinks is a similar punch coming. This is your second element in the combination. Here you deliver a fast jab, again to the head, but do not fully complete the punch; jerk it back before your opponent can make contact with it. This will cause him to overblock, leaving room for your third technique. As he overblocks, step through with your rear leg as if to change into opposite stance. As your back leg comes up, attack him to his now exposed head with reverse punch. Follow through with your final technique as your foot lands forward, which is a reverse punch to the mid-section.

*Details showing overblocking of sharply retracted punch*

## (37) Stance right to left.

This technique is most successful as a surprise attack against an opponent who keeps his weight largely on the front foot. Attack by dropping down and forward to the outside of your opponent's front foot. As you drop, bring your rear leg through, chopping away his weight-bearing front foot. This will make him fall forward on to his face. Finish with a heel kick from the floor to the back of his head.

## (38) **Stance left to left.**

One of the most effective sweeping techniques is the straightforward sweep using the rear leg against the opponent's front weight-bearing leg (*ashi-barai*). Two of the main principles in successful sweeping are to keep your supporting leg well bent, thus ensuring that you have a low centre of gravity, and to maintain a good guard with your front hand. If you do not, your opponent may have the chance to catch you with a front hand snap punch or a reverse punch. Using your front guarding hand correctly in a contra-rotating movement to your sweeping leg will also ensure that you maintain your balance. Finish with reverse punch.

## (39) **Stance left to left.**

Offer your opponent an opening by jutting your hips forward, to draw out his reverse punch. As he begins to punch withdraw your body but leave your front foot in place. When he reaches full extension hook your front foot around his front ankle and pull it towards you. This should make him fall forwards, whereupon you finish with a punch. Ensure that when you block his punch you bring your forearm right across your body, keeping your elbow well down to cover your mid-section.

## (40) **Stance right to left.**

This combination is most effective against an opponent who when under pressure retreats in a high stance and who tends to bring his feet together. As you lunge forward, bringing your rear foot across your front foot, deliver a straight punch to the head, to make him raise his guard. As his feet come together, you sweep both of his legs away with your rear leg. Finish with a heel kick or a punch.

## (41) **Stance left to left.**

Your opponent attacks with a roundhouse kick to the head. Lean back away from the kick leaving your rear arm up in front of you to make contact with his leg. Immediately his leg strikes your wrist (which should be kept relaxed until this point) your hand will automatically fold over his ankle, at which time you hook it away from you in the direction of his kick. This will spin him around, leaving his back exposed to your counter techniques.

# Chapter 11 REACTION TIME

Everyone has a unique personal reaction time – the interval between deciding upon an action and the execution of it. Obviously, in karate reaction time is vitally important. The physiological mechanism governing reaction time involves muscle fibres, motor neurones and a chemical – acetylcholine. In general a reaction takes about two tenths of a second to be initiated, but considerably longer than this if complex information has first to be interpreted. This latter, for example, occurs when a *karate-ka* falls victim to a 'feint' or 'set-up' technique.

Research carried out at Pennsylvania State University shows that when subjects were tricked into initiating an incorrect response they required some 50 per cent longer than the normal two tenths of a second to correct this response. The implication here is obvious. Time should certainly be devoted to the practice of effective 'setting-up' techniques, some of which are included in the chapter on competition techniques.

There is good evidence that an individual can speed up reaction time by practice and also enhance his or her ability to anticipate and thus have the appropriate response available. (In reaction time testing at Loughborough University, with Aidan as the subject, it was found that he had faster reflex reactions than the other sportsmen taking part.)

Of course, while you can never know in advance an opponent's techniques, good high-quality practice can give the ability to 'read' an opponent's probable strengths and weaknesses. A good coach will also be useful in reminding you of your opponent's known favourite techniques and basic style – aggressive, defensive, etc. This is one area where a good coach *is* invaluable.

Remembering the principle of specificity in training, i.e. 'you only improve at what you practise', properly designed karate-specific reaction training is essential here for sharpening up reaction time – mirror training, beating your partner to the technique, deliberately leaving an opening in your guard and reacting to your partner's attack, etc.

The moral then would appear to be that you should apportion some time in your training schedule to devising and practising some combinations which make use of 'setting-up' manoeuvres. The chapter on combination techniques gives numerous examples, and using these as a starting point you can go on to develop some of your own, using the same principles but incorporating your favourite techniques. Remember, to be effective your opponent must really believe in your 'feint' technique.

# Chapter 12 PSYCHOLOGICAL ASPECTS OF TRAINING

Lying at the heart of any -dō system is the fundamental aim to transcend the 'self' and realize the unity and interaction of the universe – a oneness inherent even within what appears on the surface to be an antagonistic encounter, for example with an opponent. This has been heavily influenced by the spread of Buddhist (and in particular Zen Buddhist) teachings – which by their nature in promoting an almost aesthetic appreciation of the transitory nature of life and the denial of the importance of personal survival, had much to commend them to the Bushi.

Many traditional martial schools (combat-orientated -jutsu ryu) began to shift their concern from that of mere survival – which was at this peaceful period in Japanese history not really a major point of consideration – to developing methods of using these martial skills in such a way as to place the emphasis more upon aesthetics than upon brutal efficiency. Thus the overriding concern became the harmony of mind and body, expressed in formal patterns of techniques (i.e. kata).

Originally these kata were developed as aids to training, ensuring that the student, even when without the personal supervision of his master, could practise a full range of basic, utilitarian defence skills. Subtly, however, the shift of concern from -jutsu to -dō became reflected in these kata. Even so, at best the kata kept alive the concept of a real opponent; although the emphasis was placed upon using kata as 'moving Zen', in that the mind and its state were as, if not more important than simple health-promoting exercises or ways of dispatching an opponent.

At one time, then, the student was to imagine every kind of combat encounter and train his body and spirit so as to emerge victorious. Now, the principle objective has become to transcend mundane consideration of winning or losing, life or death, in an attempt to enter the state of being where the karate-ka and the opponent are seen as one. As Shigeru Egami (Chief Instructor, Japan Karate-dō Shoto-kai) put it:

One enters a realm where he and his antagonist do not exist as separate individual entities; it is a world beyond egotism.
(The Way of Karate, Ward Lock Ltd, p. 42)

It is probably true to say however that this profound philosophical utilization of physical technique as a form of 'moving Zen' is seldom understood, seldom practised, very rarely persevered with, but often given as a reason (excuse) for 'pretty' but ineffectual technique and the avoidance of strong kumite – the karate-ka preferring to demonstrate tranquillity, beauty of form, suppleness and balletic athleticism as a supposed outward manifestation of zanshin.

This egoless approach to martial arts is frequently misunderstood, often considered to be solely an element of Zen meditative training, and consequently deemed as being secondary at best to a form of practice in which more pragmatic concerns such as avoiding a kick or striking an opponent are emphasized. It should be remembered, however, that many of the greatest martial warriors made use of, and indeed gave as an important factor contributing to their prowess, mental techniques drawn from Zen practice and tempered by trials of combat on the field of battle.

In The Karate-dō Manual I gave examples from the recorded sayings of some of the great Japanese swordsmen, but it would be helpful to restate here an example from one of the most renowned sword-fighters in all Japanese history: Yagyu Tajima No Kami Munenori (1571–1646).

However well a man may be trained in the art, the swordsman can never be the master of his technical knowledge unless all his psychic hindrances are removed and he can keep the mind in the state of emptiness, even purged of whatever technique he has obtained. The entire body . . . will then be capable of displaying for the first time and to its full extent all the art acquired by the training of several years . . . with the self vanishing nowhere anybody knows, the art of swordsmanship attains its perfection, and one who has it is called a genius.
(D. T. Suzuki, Zen and Japanese Culture, Princeton University Press, 1959)

Indeed, it can be claimed with some justice that Zen training was largely responsible for the Japanese success in defeating the threat of Mongol invasion in the early summer of 1281. In the peaceful years prior to the late thirteenth century, the martial skills of the Japanese fighting man had fallen into disuse and been formalized into noble but inappropriate concepts of ritualistic hand-to-hand combat. In the face of the terrifying Mongols, whose ability to instil fear into the hearts of their opponents was one of their major weapons, the Japanese learned some harsh lessons.

The outcome of this was that they instituted a Zen-based formalized system of military training in the use of the sword and the bow, thus psychologically as well as physically preparing them for the invasion which they knew was to come. In the event, in 1281, when Kublai Khan sent his invasion force of some 100,000 warriors, they found that they had been robbed of their most potent weapon. The *samurai*, with his mind disciplined by Zen exercise, had lost his fear of death. The Samurai held out unbroken against the Mongol hordes for seven weeks, when a great storm arose (Kami-kase = Divine Wind) which in two days destroyed the bulk of the enemy fleet, effectively bringing the threat of invasion to an end. Thus to dismiss the mental aspect of training is to deny aid from the tried and battle-tested experiences of many famous fighters.

This is not all, however, for the worlds of science and medicine, in particular the spheres of psychology and sport medicine, have given insights into what may loosely be called the 'Zen' approach to training, and can demonstrate that meditation, for example, can produce measurable physiological responses in the body and mind. Importantly it has been demonstrated that benefits derived from these responses are carried over into normal activity following periods of regular meditation. To give just one example: many sufferers of hypertension and raised blood pressure have found that regular meditation significantly improved their condition to the extent that drug treatment could be entirely suspended, and clinical examinations confirm these radical improvements.

That meditation, be it Transcendental, Yoga or Zen, has a measurable effect on the brain as well as the body is beyond dispute. Encephalographic measurements indicate that during meditation alpha brain wave activity predominates, followed by a shift to theta patterns (totally unlike the theta and delta patterns produced by drowsiness). Then, in advanced meditators, a stage of deep meditation produces beta waves of an almost constant amplitude and frequency. Significantly these advanced meditators continue to exhibit alpha and theta waves after the meditation has finished.

The importance of this evidence is that the presence of alpha waves indicates a state of relaxed alertness most receptive to new concepts, and conditions conducive to creativity, whilst theta waves seem to point to a state wherein the mind is capable of moments of deep insight and intuition. Albert Einstein, for example, could solve complex problems while exhibiting alpha wave activity.

Sport medicine has begun over recent years to recognize and investigate the phenomenon of the 'peak experience'. Examples abound from every imaginable sport and from such disparate athletes and sportspeople as those quoted below.

World champion racing driver Jackie Stewart:

By race time I should have no emotions inside me at all – no excitement or fear or nervousness . . . . I am absolutely cold, ice cold . . . utterly calm even though I am aware of the many things going on around me.
(*Faster: A Racer's Diary*, 1972, pp. 30–32)

Tennis champion Billie Jean King (speaking of the state of 'the effortless effort'):

It's a perfect combination of . . . violent action taking place in an atmosphere of total tranquillity . . . when it happens, I want to shout that's what it is all about! . . . . It's just having done something that's wholly pure and having experienced the perfect emotion, and I am always sad that I can't communicate that feeling . . .
(*Billie Jean*, New York 1974, p. 201)

In a special investigation for BBC Television ('The Inner Game') Peter France interviewed many well-known athletes from a variety of sporting disciplines in an attempt to find out more about the phenomenon of the 'peak experience'. The comments were illuminating.

Ian Thompson, champion marathon runner:

There is more, something else. Through physical effort athletes find a path to a sort of enlightenment very similar to those described by the Zen Buddhist, or the Yogi, in the 'peak experience' – effortless movement and concentrated attention . . . [with a] lack of judgement.

Mike Brearley, ex-England cricket captain, talks of a 'sense of oneness':

At times I felt as though the bowler's bowling and my batting were the same thing.

Arthur Ashe, 1975 Wimbledon tennis champion:

What you are trying to achieve is to empty your mind, you try to put your entire being mentally and physically on automatic pilot . . . the fewer decisions you have to consciously make the better. Sport encourages the fusion of mind and body, and helps you to reach the outer limits.

It seems beyond dispute that single-minded, intense concentration on the task in hand, through rhythmical repetitive practice and meditation, can lead to a sense of detachment, an egoless state almost exactly akin to the calm concentrated awareness – *zanshin* – of the martial arts master.

It would appear then that it is not necessary to accept Zen philosophy at all in order to obtain the physical and mental benefits which traditionally were the prerogative of the Zen student. Medical science has shown that there exist methods of increasing physical performance through a combination of specific skill activities combined with meditation and mental rehearsal techniques.

It is indeed possible to replicate the 'peak experience' effect in countless different sports and to make use of the methods of achieving this state in training schedules aimed at nothing more philosophical than becoming a champion! This is not to make any comment upon the desirability of collecting trophies, but simply to strip away the aura of mysticism that has developed – and been promoted – around the martial arts.

Any student who reads the poem *If* by Rudyard Kipling will find there a moral philosophy, a Western Zen ideal, which if followed will enable the apparent contradiction between sport and the single-minded determination to win on the one hand, and the selfless pursuit of non-competition-orientated traditional karate-dō on the other, to be resolved. Essentially competition karate can be yet another pathway towards enlightenment, if the champion can win the trophy then put it aside and move on.

## IF –

If you can keep your head when all about you
    Are losing theirs and blaming it on you,
If you can trust yourself when all men doubt you,
    But make allowance for their doubting too;
If you can wait and not be tired by waiting,
    Or being lied about, don't deal in lies,
Or being hated, don't give way to hating,
    And yet don't look too good, nor talk too wise:

If you can dream – and not make dreams your master;
    If you can think – and not make thoughts your aim;
If you can meet with Triumph and Disaster
    And treat those two impostors just the same;
If you can bear to hear the truth you've spoken
    Twisted by knaves to make a trap for fools,
Or watch the things you gave your life to, broken,
    And stoop and build 'em up with worn-out tools:

If you can make one heap of all your winnings
    And risk it on one turn of pitch-and-toss,
And lose, and start again at your beginnings
    And never breathe a word about your loss;
If you can force your heart and nerve and sinew
    To serve your turn long after they are gone,
And so hold on when there is nothing in you
    Except the Will which says to them: 'Hold on!'

If you can talk with crowds and keep your virtue,
    Or walk with Kings – nor lose the common touch,
If neither foes nor loving friends can hurt you,
    If all men count with you, but none too much;
If you can fill the unforgiving minute
    With sixty seconds' worth of distance run,
Yours is the Earth and everything that's in it,
    And – which is more – you'll be a Man, my son!

# Chapter 13 **MENTAL PREPARATION, REHEARSAL AND VISUALIZATION SKILLS**

Mental imagery is one of the most important areas in sports today.

So states Dr Patricia Mihevic, psychologist at the University of California, Santa Barbara. (Quoted in J. Fixx, p. 49)

*Coach, Athlete and the Sports Psychologist* cites the example of Robert Foster, a champion rifle shot, who because of military duties was unable to train for a whole year. During this period his only practice was a daily ten-minute session of mental rehearsal and visualization. At the end of the year he entered a competition and broke his own world record.

Jean-Claude Killy, three times gold medal winning skier, was unable to practise for one event because of injury. The only practice he got was to ski the course in his imagination. In his opinion that event saw him give one of his best ever performances.

Chuck Norris, top US *karate-ka* and movie star:

When I entered a competition I never felt stress because I was physically, psychologically and mentally prepared.

To eliminate stress from your consciousness you must be prepared to handle any contingency that may arise. You should concentrate on the task at hand and visualize the result you want.

(Extract from *The Secret of Inner Strength*)

Lee Evans, 1968 Olympic 400 metres champion who also set a world record which lasted for over ten years, prepared for the Olympic event by repeatedly visualizing each stride he would take until his performance improved.

Arnold Schwarzenegger, one of the world's greatest body-builders, would first visualize the effect that he wanted in a muscle from a series of exercises, and maintain that mental image while carrying out his routine.

Jack Nicklaus explains how he mentally views a film-like sequence showing the entirety of an action from initial swing to the ball lying exactly where he wants it. He stresses, however, the need for the internal movie to show the 'perfect shot'.

# Vince

My own experience may be helpful here. Some fifteen years ago I remember beginning to use visualization as part of my karate training. At first I would lie in bed at night going through in my mind the various techniques that I had been practising with my teacher during the day, trying to understand them and to comprehend the essence of the technique. I would concentrate on particular parts of the training session which had not gone well for me, and by continually replaying the scene in my mind's eye try to understand where the problem lay and thus gain some notion as to how to correct the fault. After some while I was able to conjure up a minute figure of myself in my imagination, and of my partners or opponents, and then replay the action almost like rerunning a video film over and over again.

It occurred to me that it might be helpful to incorporate this into my meditation practice and consciously attempt to correct the faults in the sequence, or on the video as it were, and thus rectify the problem. I began then to move from my meditation practice – in which I would merely

follow my breathing – into actual visualization practice wherein I would see in my mind my own self in miniature complete with *karate-gi*, just like watching a small TV picture. This figure would then do the technique exactly as I would imagine myself doing it, complete with mistakes. I would then analyse the mistakes and set about correcting them in this little mental 'alter ego'. Still relaxed and breathing calmly, but concentrating firmly on the little figure, I would then rerun the technique slowly, eradicating the faults. Then I would begin to speed the action up and would do it time and time again until I became convinced that that was how I always did and always would do the technique.

At this stage I was somewhat disconcerted to find that when I really 'got into' this practice my heart rate would increase and I would actually start to feel the technique as if I were physically doing it, although at one stage removed. (Latterly I discovered that this 'living the technique' was indeed beneficial, and was to be encouraged.) I would feel the excitement, I would feel the rise in the spirit and I would feel the actuality of the technique. I would keep this practice up for only a short period initially, and if I found my attention wavered I relaxed and let go, returning to simple meditation and calm breathing. I found that in general from five to ten minutes spent on a particular visualization technique was sufficient.

I was not at that time a particularly supple person and the training regime which I was following did nothing to change this (hence the section on stretching in this book), but I always was an aggressive fighter, with strong sweeps (from my years in judo), front kicks and strong punches. I began to find, however, that my speed was not all that it should have been, so I began to look for ways in which to improve it.

I took to heart Asano Sensei's advice to have a 'stone face' – that is, never to telegraph one's intentions by any little giveaway signs – and I would practise in front of a large mirror at my university *dojo*. I would attempt to beat my reflection to the punch! And I would do it by not attempting to think of when to punch, but simply letting my body think for itself; in other words, the punch punched.

Following this I would meditate briefly and relax and visualize myself as usual, but this time facing an opponent. I would then see my opponent move fractionally and whatever the technique I would see myself immediately attack so hard and fast as to stop that opponent dead in his tracks! I would do this time and time again in my head.

The final step was to transfer the mental image to physical practice, first in one-step sparring and then free-sparring. The end result of this practice was that my ability to catch an opponent right at the instant of his attack was vastly improved and I gained much success from this.

From these initial experiments I soon learned that if I set specific but achievable goals in my visualization practice, I was soon able to see the results. For example, I began to improve my *mawashi-geri* by making the image in my mind perform the technique correctly and effortlessly at middle (*chudan*) level; then, as my flexibility increased because of my on-going flexibility and stretching training programme, I increased the height of my mental self's kick. I continued this practice until I was able to execute the kick at head (*jodan*) height.

Further research has shown that it is important to approach a major goal in a series of short steps. Do not immediately set yourself a task which is physically way beyond your capabilities. As your karate training is for life, you should approach your main goal with a series of milestones along the way, so to speak. Concentrate on achieving your goals, thus beginning a success feedback loop which will add to your self-confidence.

As you concentrate on watching yourself performing in your imagination, try to establish a deep conviction that the tiny image is actually you.

Try to experience the feel of the technique and perhaps hear yourself 'ki-ai'. Under these conditions it can be shown that when a person effectively visualizes physical activity, the nervous system actually does convey tiny signals to the muscles. In an experiment some runners were asked to lie down and without moving imagine that they were running up a steep hill. They were wired up to an electromyograph, which measured muscle movement. Although no physical movement was seen, the machine recorded electrical activity in the muscles used in running.

Visualization also serves to cut short the learning process and facilitate the sending of the impulses from the brain to the muscles and back again. After all, the ultimate learning of skills, and the eradication of bad technique or habits, occurs in the brain; for it is the brain that organizes the movements of the body.

The visualization technique should be practised regularly and frequently in small doses. Five to ten minutes at least five days a week is far better than twenty minutes once a week. Actually there is no reason why five minutes spent in seated meditation (*seiza*) before every training period could not be used for this visualization practice.

As mentioned before, your training in karate should be seen as a lifelong commitment. This being so, then naturally your mental approach will differ in line with your age and ability: the former regularly increasing, the latter following a curve of increase followed by general gradual decline. It would be inappropriate to set the same physical goals throughout this life plan – they should be in line with what is possible, not unrealistic. Although it is fair to say that few, if any of us actually fully realize our potential.

Again, during this life plan it will be necessary to adjust the mental approach in line with whatever short-term goal is aimed for. The competition *karate-ka*, for instance, would do better to design a structured pattern of training in order to 'peak' for specific events. This will entail a somewhat different approach to that of the *karate-ka* for whom competition features only as a small element of regular training in the classical way.

I must stress once more, however, that to discriminate too emphatically between the two stereotypes is wrong; what matters is the purpose for which each way is followed. Both types should share common aims, which can be summed up briefly as:

(1) Freedom from fear and tension, allowing unrestricted appropriate physical action in combat, competition or everyday life.
(2) Freedom from ego and its restricting influences in both physical activity and mental/spiritual terms.
(3) To realize the physical potential which arises from the harmonizing of mind and body.

# Chapter 14 BEGINNING MENTAL VISUALIZATION AND TRAINING

There are a number of problems which the *karate-ka* must overcome in order to achieve the aims outlined above. These problems fall into two broad groups; physical and mental. Examples of the former are injury, lack of form, poor technique and lack of experience, while in the latter group fall anxiety, inability to relax, loss of concentration, etc. Obviously the problems in the first of these groups can be overcome by direct actions such as continual practice in correcting a weak technique, by beginning a programme of weight training to facilitate recovery from injury, and such like. The second group is that to which we will pay most attention here.

All anxiety is accompanied by physical tension. A certain degree of tension can be beneficial in that it leads to a state of positive arousal which enhances performance, but an unreasonable amount of physical tension can lead to the inhibition of correct physical response. This in itself can lead to the competitor or the *karate-ka* being unable to fulfil his desire to perform effectively and efficiently, thus creating more anxiety, and so the feedback loop continues.

Some of this anxiety, however, can almost be placed in category one, as it is essentially to do with stress originating from causes which can be directly the result of physical environment, and can therefore be alleviated by physical means. The competition venue, for example, is often an unfamiliar environment and can unsettle a competitor, as can a hostile audience, not to mention strange hotel rooms, unusual foods, unfamiliar languages and so on; all of which the top-class competitor will have to cope with.

The answer is if possible to try to see the venue before the event and get the feel of it. Virginia Wade, 1977 Wimbledon tennis champion, would go to the court in the morning before the match to attune herself to the area and its surroundings. When the USSR began to find that its teams were being faced with hostile receptions in the West, their coaches instituted home practices to the sound of booing and jeering blasting out from loudspeakers. For major events, particularly internationals, it is generally the practice to have teams and competitors arrive a few days early in order to acclimatize themselves to the conditions and to become familiar with the actual competition area.

If it is not physically possible to visit the competition venue, then it is even more important that the competitor is able to feel comfortable in any environment because his or her training has included an element of mental preparation which will allow concentration to be on the 'self' and inward rather than outward and open to distraction.

As an aid to this it is useful to vary the direction that you face when you carry out your normal training programme. Most *dojos* follow a prescribed pattern which is invariable. It is therefore useful to break the pattern. Train facing a different direction to the usual; train in a different part of the *dojo*; try to train in different *dojos*. Try to become more aware of yourself rather than paying too much attention to external influences.

Aidan trains a lot to music, and he found this particularly useful in the midst of the great tension of the World Championships in Tokyo. By playing the music on a personal headset Aidan was able to cut off the external distractions and to feel at home by mental concentration, relaxation and the aural stimulation from the music which would evoke familiar memories and feelings in an otherwise unfamiliar and hostile environment. We shall look more at this later.

If we move on to another element in the mental category of problems to be overcome, there is the number one enemy of uninhibited action – fear. Fear of an opponent, fear of losing face, fear of letting down the side/team/club/coach/family etc. – the list is endless.

Remember that fear, like anxiety, manifests itself in physical terms closely akin to excitement, and the fight or flight response can be a useful physiological condition to evoke; but it should be a controlled and controllable response channelled into the correct pathways. Fear and tension allowed to have free rein ungoverned by reason and confident anticipation can only be harmful. There are of course exercises, deep breathing and relaxation which can help to alleviate the symptoms of this response. It is useful however to look at one of the main problems here in isolation prior to the turmoil of an actual competition event itself.

Psychologists point out that fear of rejection – our concern for what others may think of us if we fail or let the team or *sensei* down – is at the heart of almost all worry. Simply put, in most spheres of life – including and often most evident in competitive situations – an over-active concern for other people's opinions can actually give rise to the tension which inhibits performance and thus goes a long way towards realizing the very fears which caused the problem in the first place.

The solution is fairly simple. Most importantly it is based upon our acceptance of ourselves and our personal worth regardless of other people's opinions.

To thine own self be true, and it shall follow as the night the day, thou canst not then be false to any man.
(Polonius' advice to Laertes, *Hamlet*, W. Shakespeare)

Of course this may not be easy to achieve, but various methods may help. One technique is simply to reduce the problem to absurdity. Imagine the worst possible outcome of any event which is troubling you. If you lose will your marriage end in divorce, will you be ostracized by the community, will your parents or children refuse to speak to you, must you leave home? The sheer ludicrousness will help to put things in their proper perspective. It should also help to dwell upon the truism that the anticipation of a problem is always worse than dealing with the actual problem itself.

Having made the point that fear can undermine and inhibit the performance of even the best athlete, it should be apparent that instilling fear in the mind of an opponent is a stratagem as old as warfare itself.

The first occidental Olympic judo champion, the giant Dutchman Anton Geesink, many times European Open-weight gold medallist, in the week before the start of the 1964 judo competition found out where the Japanese team were carrying out their training. Then, having also discovered the time of the training sessions, Geesink got up even earlier and made sure that they saw him all covered in sweat coming in from his training before they had even started theirs.

At the first Shotokan Karate International World Champions the Japanese team began their usual group warming-up routine, which served also to refocus themselves mentally in the unfamiliar surroundings and to have a demoralizing effect on the opposition. Seeing this, Aidan went over to the group, and right next to them began his own warming-up routine, treating them to a close-up display of his punching and kicking abilities. After a while the Japanese group dispersed!

What we are really saying at this stage is that once the physical skill level is at its optimum, it becomes vitally important that the mental side of training is given due emphasis and not neglected or deemed to be unimportant.

*The faces of the team reflect the tension of competition*

The athlete who effectively utilizes his or her mental strength becomes stronger and develops greater personal control.

(Tony Orlick, *Psyching for Sport*, p. 2, Leisure Press 1986)

To begin this programme of mental training you must first realistically assess your starting point: your current skill levels, your strengths and weaknesses, and the level of your commitment to sticking to the programme once initiated. If you are technically a good *karate-ka*, fit and flexible with a good range of skills, and yet often unsuccessful in competition, there is little point in going back to practise more techniques or even gain greater fitness unless the losses are the result of basic inadequacies in these aspects. Far better spend your time on creating a systematic positive 'mind-set', a focus of concentration both before the event and within it, for it is likely that this practice will be more beneficial.

If at this stage of your karate career your ambition is to be successful in competition, your training and visualization should serve to prepare you for what you have to do in competition, not for what you have to do in your training. If your basic aim is to enhance your pragmatic combat efficiency, then techniques suitable to this end should form the basis of your visualization. The goals set should be specific to the aims which reflect your current ambitions and should essentially enable you to refine your ability to concentrate and minimize the effects of distractions.

Silvi Berneir, springboard diver and gold medallist in the 1984 Olympics, set herself an intensive programme of visualization in the lead-up to the Games. In her practice she rehearsed each dive again and again, and on the day she concentrated on taking each dive at a time, just as in her visualization, and between dives, like Aidan, she cut herself off from her surroundings by listening to a music tape, thus reinforcing the feeling of familiarity and of things 'going to plan'.

If you are using your visualization practice for a specific event, it would perhaps pay to remember that it is not always beneficial to set your visualization sights upon winning the medal. Rather concentrate on what you have to do in order to win, thus establishing goals which are directly within your control and are therefore achievable. In other words, the actual decision in any event is not always within your control as a bad referee's decision can rob you of a victory which should have been yours and a trophy which should have been yours. This is beyond your powers to control. It is far more beneficial to concentrate upon visualization techniques aimed at enabling you to perform at the level of skill and proficiency which would, all else being equal, enable you to be a medal winner. This goal is certainly attainable and within your control.

To begin any journey it is necessary to know the starting point. So it is with developing a programme of mental visualization training. Some authorities recommend the drawing up of self-assessment charts, one detailing medium- and long-term goals which is used for overall training assessment, and one specifically designed for performance assessment. Of the two I feel that the latter performance-related type can be of invaluable help in analysing the mental activity before, during and after both successful and unsuccessful events, so as to aid recognition of success-enhancing patterns in order to re-create them consistently.

Regularly compiled and consulted, these records can also help the *karate-ka* to recognize and avoid those mental attitudes which bring about negative results. It is therefore helpful if a short record of every competition is kept either by the *karate-ka* or the coach, detailing such things as feelings and emotions before the event on a scale of 0 to 10 as follows.

0 – mentally and physically low, to
10 – mentally and physically high

0 – no worries or anxieties, to
10 – extremely anxious and worried

0 – no ability to focus or keep concentration, to
10 – absolute and complete focus and concentration, etc.

It also helps to note down what was going through your mind immediately prior to the match – any particular positive or negative feelings about specifics, for example the size of an opponent, the noise of the crowd, the abilities of the referees, whether or not you have beaten or been beaten by this opponent before, and so on.

Tony Orlick in his excellent work *Psyching for Sport* points out:

When I looked closely at the worst performances of highly skilled athletes, I found that they were almost always preceded by negative self-suggestions.

All this self-analysis will enable you to construct a positive mental routine which must be practised time and again and which is automatically set into operation at every event. You or your coach should ensure that the debriefing is carried out as soon as possible after each match finishes. Even if, after a loss or a poor performance, you do not feel that you want to be bothered with this, force yourself! Learn from your setbacks; the information gained by such analysis is invaluable.

During the pre-contest periods you must also develop the habit of mentally rehearsing the feelings of a good performance, when all seemed to go right with you. In other words, develop your own refocusing routine by reminding yourself of what it felt like when you were on top form, and how good you feel now knowing that you have done the training and are both physically and psychologically in superb condition. Remind yourself also that the goals you have set (to allow techniques to flow powerfully and naturally, with confidence and speed etc.) are within your control and you can achieve them.

You should also establish the type of physical warm-up routine which works best for you and go through it every time you prepare for a contest. This too will give a positive feedback and lead to the knowledge that things are under your control. It may help if you use music to distance yourself from all distractions and re-create a pattern once more within your control and in your own little universe.

Continue to use these mental and physical routines to establish your own area of concern within all that is going on around you, and use it again and again to refocus should any distractions occur. Do not let tiredness or frustration distract you from your refocusing routines.

Olympic gold medal-winning athlete David Hemery gives a very good example of a refocusing technique which certainly seemed to work for him. Just before his Olympic final in Mexico, while changing into his spikes, he saw the pre-race favourite practise his starts and fly off at great speed. Hemery felt the first stages of panic, and realizing that it was important to maintain his sense of personal control left his running shoes off and ran at an easy pace on the wet grass at the side of the track. This took him back to the sensation of his practice runs in shallow water on the sands in Massachusetts. He imagined the sun on his back and felt the sensation of his body flowing with health and strength. This image was so strong that it actually blanked out the feeling of panic that he had started to experience and helped put his mind back into a strong and positive condition. Of course, history now tells us that Hemery went on to win that Olympic gold medal!

Having established from your post-competition records the type of mental mind-set which is beneficial to you and which you recognize as accompanying success in any event, it is essential that you realize that there are two distinct areas of concern in designing your mental approach. The first deals with pre-competition training and build-up, and the second specifically centres on the competition itself.

Area number one is based upon critical self-analysis and the development of physical and mental programmes to promote confidence in your technical ability and self-esteem through goal setting and achievement as directed by the mental visualization rehearsal and concentration techniques.

Number two, being more event specific, is more concerned with the focusing of the mind on positive elements and creating a feedback loop of confident awareness by channelling the natural nervousness and anxiety away from inhibiting and self-defeating tension into positive, beneficial and performance-enhancing arousal.

If you wish to be a good, successful, competitive fighter then it is vital that you are prepared to enter many events, not initially with perhaps any great hope of winning but for two main reasons, both psychological. First you should learn to let the success or failure of an event rest for you not upon whether or not you win a medal but on whether or not you achieve your own goal. Set your sights on what is within your grasp and your control. Secondly, even the best designed form of training can never take the place of the real thing. You must become familiar with the patterns of competition: the travelling involved, the variety of venues and changing facilities, the tactics of other competitors, the feel of the crowd . . . and so on. You will then find that the stress factor diminishes and these events will become normal to you.

Finally, before moving on to a more detailed explanation of the technique of mental rehearsal and visualization, remember that although you may find that you are dealing with an aspect of training which might be unfamiliar to you, by following the steps outlined you will be able to learn the mental skills just as readily as you have been able to learn the physical ones.

# The technique

This section gives a step-by-step introduction to meditation and to the techniques of mental rehearsal and visualization. In moments of great tension it is useful to have a technique available to you which will help to calm the nerves and bring your body back under your control. Meditation techniques of deep regular slow breathing, combined with either concentration upon a mantra or particular image, or indeed simply upon the act of breathing itself, have been used for thousands of years in just this sort of situation.

These techniques are just as useful to the *karate-ka* but they cannot be used properly without practice. Therefore we advise that all *karate-ka* spend at least some of their time in meditation. This of course is anyway a useful adjunct to hard training, not only because it will afford practice in relaxing through slow and regular breathing, which can then be brought into service at any time in moments of stress, but because of the physical well-being which it will promote.

You should always begin your mental visualization

and rehearsal with just such a short period of relaxation and meditation in order to calm the nervous system and allow it more easily to process and assimilate the new information it will gather from the practice. This learning process, being mental rather than physical, is of a more subtle nature and could be negated by physical activity undertaken at the same time.

Basic rule number one: **make time!** It will take time for these techniques to be learned and therefore you must be ruthless in allotting yourself a regular period every day for practice. Half an hour will suffice.

Make sure that you are wearing comfortable loose-fitting clothing, and that you can have access to a quiet private place where you will not be disturbed by either people or outside activity. If it is possible – at least initially – to darken the room somewhat, so much the better. In this particular meditation I recommend that you keep your eyes closed. In meditation proper this is not absolutely necessary, but it will be necessary for the visualization and rehearsal techniques which will follow.

Do not meditate on either a full or an empty stomach. Either condition can lead to distraction.

While you do not have to be able to sit in the full lotus position, I recommend that you make use of a cushion and either sit cross-legged on it if you are able, or place it between the heels to support the buttocks and kneel in the sieza position if your hips and legs are not very flexible. The main point is to sit erect, almost with the feeling that someone is pulling upwards on the top of your head. Tuck in your chin slightly, rest your hands upon your thighs, one on top of the other thumbs touching or simply palms down on the top of your thighs, but not with the elbows sticking out, and do not have fists clenched. Practise this position, remembering periodically to check that your spine is still erect, not slumping over as time goes on.

While there are many techniques for quietening the mind, one of the simplest and most useful is just counting breaths. When in the correct position take two or three deep breaths and let them out slowly, relaxing the limbs more with each exhalation. Quietly begin to notice the way in which your stomach swells on each breath intake and deflates on each exhalation. Do not try to establish any forced pattern of breathing, just sit quietly and watch until your own personal pattern is established.

At this stage some five minutes will have passed and your breaths will be fairly slow and regular. (Do remember though that you should still be feeling the breath inflating your abdomen rather than your chest.) Now mentally count 'one' as you breathe in. Let the breath out naturally and easily. Now count 'two' on the next inspiration, and so on until you reach the count of ten. At this stage just return to the beginning and start the count again.

This practice is to calm your mind, so do not force it to concentrate. If you find that thoughts occur to you and distract your attention from watching and counting your breaths, do not get angry with yourself; simply begin again at the first count. This is not an easy discipline but eventually it becomes possible to concentrate the mind more fully on the task in hand.

I find that students – and in particular Western students – generally need quite a lot of will-power to persevere with this practice, as they seem to feel the need to fill every moment of their lives with activity, if not physical then at least mental. Ask what they do for relaxation and most people will reel off a list of activities: reading, playing tennis, watching the television, drinking – the list is infinite. What they term 'relaxing' is more often than not the exchanging of one activity for another.

It is important for the martial artist to have moments of quiet stillness and introspection in order to reach his centre, from which life and its trials and tribulations can be set into proper perspective. If you cannot be in control in moments of quietness, how can you expect to have this control in moments of extreme stress? Regular short periods of practice, however, will soon enable anyone who continues in spite of the difficulties to master this deceptively simple exercise.

The final stage is to be attempted only when you can consistently count your breaths without major distraction for a period of five minutes. When you reach this point simply stop counting, stop watching and sit, calmly and quietly. At this stage EEG measurement of the brain waves will normally demonstrate a preponderance of alpha (8 to 14 cycles per second) activity, which is indicative of relaxed alertness and of a state in which the brain seems most receptive.

As an aside, I would like to point out that in my opinion all *karate-ka* would benefit enormously from practising meditation as an end in itself, and if they could reach the simply sitting stage and do it daily for even twenty minutes, they would undoubtedly reap the benefits. These, while primarily concerning the philosophical aims of Zen – a fuller understanding of 'self' and the relationships between 'self' and the universe – also include the more mundane, such as the well-being induced by periods of complete rest, deeper even than sleep, and physiological changes such as rapid reduction in anxiety levels.

Tests show that meditation can bring about a significant decrease in the level of blood lactate, a substance which appears to have strong connections with symptoms of anxiety which occur in stressful situations. Other benefits include lower resting levels of blood pressure, a lower resting heart rate and a decrease in hypertension.

At the moment, however, this whole procedure of sitting and watching is simply a preparatory stage in the visualization technique. After this short meditation period we can begin to work on the mental rehearsal and visualization routine itself. Following the points discussed earlier, you will have assessed the problem area to be worked upon and set an achievable but not too easy goal to work towards.

As an example let us take a simple technique that you are trying to groove into your reflexive repertoire – perhaps front snap kick (*mae-geri keage*). Begin by projecting a tiny figure (don't attempt to put features on it) on the blank screen of your mind. Imagine the figure wearing the same apparel that you normally wear in practice, and see the figure standing in a free stance, well balanced and powerful.

Play the first move of the sequence at a medium speed and watch the figure snap up the front knee and follow the kick as it whips out. Watch the figure maintain its balance and withdraw the foot sharply before resuming the well-balanced stance. Now do it again, correcting any tendency for the figure to lean backwards, or drop the hands, or fail to return to a strong stance.

At this stage you can now begin to project your own identity into the figure. There is no need to see your own features in detail; the figure will mould itself to your basic physical characteristics, and you will 'know' that it is you.

Now you can imagine this figure (you) doing the technique as you normally do it, paying attention to any particular faults in the technique that you know you are prone to and which prevent you from performing the technique perfectly. Perhaps, for example, you do not in actual practice bring up your front knee high enough. So watch your alter ego perform the kick and then begin to correct it. Watch yourself start to bring up the knee to a higher point before snapping out the leg, and repeat this process a few times still at medium speed.

At this point, maintaining your concentration on the figure, increase the speed of the technique and repeat it until you can see it in your mind at optimum speed and without faults. Begin to hear the snap of the *gi*, and the sharp exhalation of breath with each technique. Repeat this at least 10 to 15 times. Until you are fairly well practised in the technique it will take you some minutes to reach this stage, so initially halt the mental rehearsal practice after 8 to 10 minutes (15 in total with the preliminary meditation/relaxation).

This practice can be carried out anywhere and at any time that you have a few minutes to spare. I used to spend a few minutes going through techniques like this in bed before going to sleep.

After a while, when your visualization technique has improved, you can begin to incorporate it into your physical practice period.

Find a quiet place in the *dojo* where you can be undistracted and spend five minutes in relaxed meditation, followed by five minutes mentally rehearsing the technique you wish to practise. Immediately following the mental rehearsal assume the same stance as the figure in your mind and, at medium speed, follow exactly the same pattern of practice, concentrating without any physical tension on the same points as rehearsed, lifting the knee high, maintaining a good guard, snapping the leg out and back and assuming a good strong stance and so on.

Do not allow any negative thoughts to intrude. You have 'seen' yourself doing it, so you know that you can do it. Increase the speed a little at a time, but keep relaxed, and each time regain the same strong, relaxed, balanced stance as the little mental figure. Holding yourself briefly in this relaxed free stance position, close your eyes and re-run the technique again in your mind. You will find that this will now be relatively easy.

Now do the technique physically. Now rehearse it mentally. Now do the technique physically, and so on. As the technique starts to become grooved into your body and mind you can project the figure with *kime* and *ki-ai*, hearing and feeling the completeness of the action. Then immediately repeat the process physically.

One word of warning. Do not continually repeat this exercise until you reach the stage where your technique begins to deteriorate through tiredness, as this will lead to a discrepancy between the performance of the mental image and the physical actuality, and could result in a sense of failure in the practice, which would be a stumbling block towards progress. Much better keep the practice short and selective and end it at the point where real physical improvement occurs.

This is the basic principle of mental rehearsal, and as fluency increases you will find that it is easy to include an opponent in the action and rehearse quite complex manoeuvres and tactics. Again, although it may seem to take quite a long time to read about, the whole process should not last more than some 12 to 15 minutes in total but should be practised daily, and can be carried out even when it is not possible to follow the mental rehearsal with the physical practice. There is a vast amount of evidence to confirm that this mental visualization and rehearsal programme can have extremely beneficial effects and should certainly become part of a serious *karate-ka*'s practice.

# Summary

(1) Analyse your motivation, skill levels, strengths and weaknesses.

(2) Design your personal assessment charts.

(3) Set realistic short-term goals, continually resetting them as they are achieved.

(4) Begin regular practice of relaxation and meditation routine.

(5) When proficient at this extend it into specific visualization and rehearsal routine.

(6) Follow visualization rehearsal by physical practice of same technique.

(7) Practice the visualization rehearsal routine every day until the image is clear and sharp and can be easily called up.

(8) Continue to set testing but achievable goals so as to reinforce the success feedback loop to promote self confidence further.

(9) Prepare and practice a refocusing technique by concentrating on visualizing your best performances and reminding yourself about how strong, fit, sharp and well-prepared you are. Use this refocus routine during each competition.

(10) Following competition analyse your feelings before and during the event and record any significant differences between successful and unsuccessful matches. Make use of this information in designing your mental practice priorities. If, for example, these post-competition assessments indicate a problem in loss of concentration, then simply returning to a physical training schedule will be useless.

In conclusion, do not dismiss this mental side of karate lightly. Do read further on the subject – some useful books are recommended in the Appendix.

Both Aidan and I feel that what we are drawing attention to in this chapter is not essentially new to martial arts, but is perhaps a more easily understandable explanation of what may be obscured in terms like 'hara', 'spirit', 'Zen mind' and so on. We have concentrated in this chapter on extremely mundane reasons for bringing the mind into karate practice. This is not to undervalue the philosophical benefits from so doing. Plato in his *Republic*:

. . . there are the consequences of hard bodily exercise and high living, with no attempt to cultivate the mind or use the intellect in study. At first, the sense of physical fitness fills a man with self-confidence and energy and makes him twice the man that he was. But suppose he holds himself aloof from any sort of culture; then, even if there is something in him capable of desiring knowledge, it is starved of instruction and never encouraged to think for itself . . . and so it grows feeble for lack of stimulus and nourishment, and deaf and blind because the darkness that clouds perception is never cleared away. Such a man ends by being wholly uncultivated and a hater of reason.

Having no more use for reasonable pursuasion, he gains his ends by savage violence, like a brute beast and he lives in dull stupor of ignorance with no touch of inward harmony or grace.

The final part of this section deals with Aidan's success in the World Championships in Tokyo, showing how he was helped by the use of mental rehearsal focusing and refocusing techniques.

# Chapter 15 AIDAN – BACKGROUND TO A WORLD TITLE

Looking back over my preparations for the World Championships in Tokyo, I was surprised to see just how much importance and emphasis I had placed on the mental side of my training. At the time I had not really researched much into the psychological aspects of training and most of what I did just seemed so natural. Only looking back can I see the obvious similarities between my instinctive approach and carefully planned mental rehearsal and preparation.

During my training I was continually setting myself goals. For example, I was never too keen on running and did not consider myself to be a good runner. I began training with some good distance runners who were all physically better adapted to the sport than I. My plan was to pick the best runner and to try to stay with him all the way, and use my explosive sprinting power in the final few metres. To my astonishment (and to theirs) I did this, and won! Not once, but on three or four occasions! Obviously I was very fit from all my other training (circuits, weights, sparring in a lead vest etc.) but I believe it was my total concentration and the way I could focus all my attention on using this as a step towards the World Championships that made the difference.

Because of my enthusiasm I actually began my training schedule a good month before the rest of the squad. This early general fitness training allowed me to spend more time towards the end of the programme to work on technique. The early preparation also showed while training with other members of the team. When we were doing circuit training I would always make achieving the best time through the circuit my sole aim. So in the sprint training, I would always be determined to win, and win I did.

I would also boost my self-confidence in other ways. For example, I had made a point of going running with my training partner on Christmas Day and as we ran we would mention our rivals and joke 'I bet he is tucking into Christmas dinner now!' – and little did he think that we were out training. This was not at all a run for physical fitness! I was already in good shape. This was purely to obtain a sense of psychological 'one-upmanship'. These minor victories seemed to build up a sort of 'bank balance' of credit, from which I was able to draw extra confidence when I was under pressure.

Again, during my training I used music a lot. In particular I used music that was exciting and had a strong rhythm and beat (actually 'Eye of the Tiger' was one of my favourites). I would use music while doing circuits and sparring and practising my technique in order to cut out everything else and help me concentrate on keeping my mind focused on what I was doing, especially when I was beginning to tire.

During the World Championships I would put on my personal stereo player and just lose myself in the music. This enabled me to isolate myself from all the unfamiliarity and keep my link with home. Forgetting that I was half a world away, I was back in familiar surroundings visualizing my techniques. As I got closer to the final, the pressure became more intense. Well-wishers, thinking that they were being helpful, kept coming up to me and telling me that I had to win, as everyone was relying on me in the face of the Japanese domination. At this point it seemed to me that I was walking a mental tightrope. One part of me was trying to remain calm and keep things in perspective, while another part of me wanted to forget the whole thing and just go home!

My body was strong and fit, I was in top physical shape, and my techniques were fast and strong. So what could go wrong? My mind! I could feel that unless I kept my mental attitude right I could blow it all! The answer was to forget about the final. I refused to think of winning or losing a world trophy and concentrated only on the next fight, that opponent and my strategy for beating him.

Before the quarter-final match I went into the corridor and was just carrying out my stretching and warming-up routine in preparation for the match, which was an extremely important one against the Japanese golden boy Kasuya. At this point my instructor Asano Sensei came to me and began to tell me what I should do in the next fight. This surprised me very much as Asano Sensei never coached any of his students at championships. As I had already decided what my strategy would be and what tactics I would use, the advice that Sensei gave me would not have worked. That does not mean that it was wrong, but that it was just not right for me. The point is, however, that Sensei had come to help and encourage me at a very critical time, and this really did give me a psychological boost.

As a matter of fact the refereeing was so bad on occasions during this event that had it not been for Asano Sensei's protestations I would actually have been disqualified. (Unfortunately this standard was

Opposite: *Aidan:* yoko tobi geri

*Aidan and Asano with the World Championship trophy*

with my knees and punch him twice more . . . full point!

Now it was time for the semi-final match, and I was up against another top Japanese fighter. The atmosphere was electric. I found a quiet private place and sat there for a few minutes where no one could see me, to calm my whirling thoughts. I was alone, and was able to show my nervousness and anxiety. I began once again to refocus on the fight.

With four minutes to go I was back out in the arena, still with my headphones on. I was mentally keyed up, yet physically relaxed. I did not try to 'psych out' my opponent through eye contact or aggressive displays as some fighters do. He already knew what I could do, and I felt that that was sufficient. As I listened to the music I kept running through techniques in my mind. I could see myself punching him, kicking him. I was faster than him, always beating him to the punch. I told myself that I had worked harder than him, I had sweated more, and taken all the pain, and I deserved to win. Not until the last seconds did I take off the headphones and step on to the mat.

As it turned out, this fight, although full of tension, was something of an anti-climax as my opponent never even got a chance to throw a technique. I had noticed that many of the Japanese fighters had a basic fault in that they tended to keep their hands too low. My opponent here was exactly the same, and by doing one or two small feints to bring his hands even further down I knew that he would never be able to stop a fast kick to the head. So it was. In less than 20 seconds I caught him smack on the side of the head with a reverse front foot roundhouse kick for a full point and the match. Again, following this I went away from the turmoil and refocused myself mentally.

Before I knew it I was on the mat for the final event of the whole Championships against the top Japanese fighter Sugimoto. This was the final chance for any non-Japanese to win a gold medal.

The fight started with us both testing each other out. I attacked with a strong punching combination but Sugimoto was very fast and leapt backwards. Nevertheless I caught him with what I knew to be a good solid punch to the body. To my astonishment the Japanese referee and the four Japanese judges all failed to see my technique and instead awarded Sugimoto a half point for a punch delivered as he was jumping backwards! In spite of this my concentration never wavered, and I ignored his point.

I found that Sugimoto was a defensive fighter. I stamped my foot hard on to the mat and he leapt backwards, anticipating an attack. Suddenly an opening appeared during an exchange of techniques and I swept both of his legs cleanly, punching him on the way down. As soon as the referee saw the sweep, however, he yelled stop, so my punch could not score. (This happened many

maintained at the next World Championships in Dusseldorf, but on that occasion Asano Sensei's intervention was ignored.)

Interestingly I actually won the World Championships wearing one of Asano Sensei's *gis*, as mine was covered in blood from a severe cut in the mouth that I had received earlier on. After the Championships Asano gave me the *gi* to keep as a souvenir.

Anyway, in the match I drew out Kasuya's techniques, and as he launched an attack I slid in and caught him with front foot *yoko-geri* to the mid-section. This gained a half-point score. Kasuya had been watching me all day scoring with front foot reverse roundhouse kicks, and I knew that he had figured out his strategy to deal with this by moving in on me. Because I was aware of this, I was able to fool him into thinking that when I lifted my knee high I was going to attack with a reverse roundhouse; he leapt in, straight on to my side thrust kick. Kasuya was now under pressure to bring the fight to me, and as he kept edging forward I kept my body weight back, and my left hand up as a guard. Then, using my back foot, I swept him over, punching him as he went. Because I knew where he was going to fall I was able to control him

*Aidan with the world-famous actor, Toshiro Mifune, at the World Championships in Tokyo*

times during the Championships, indeed three times during this very fight, with the referee intervening too quickly, not giving time for the technique to be finished.)

We were both moving around the area a lot. Sugimoto kept trying to meet my punches by jumping into the air and counter punching. I feinted and he did just this, upon which I caught him in mid-air with a strong *mae-geri* (front kick) to level the score. Time was called, the match ended and was adjudged a draw.

An extension was ordered. As it started I swept his front foot and punched to the head. This was ignored by the referee. I immediately did it again, but swept both of his feet. Once again the referee ignored it. At this stage Sugimoto tried to provoke me into attacking him so that he could counter me. He began to wave his hand at me and give me an obvious opening. I did just the opposite, however, and dropped my own guard to give him a chance which he could not refuse. He immediately attacked with front kick, but I was ready for him and side-stepped to catch him with a reverse punch

that the referee could not ignore.

During the next exchange I once more swept and punched him. I was by now not surprised at the lack of response from the referee. I left my front foot forward as bait, and Sugimoto, just as I wanted, tried to sweep me. This was a foolish mistake as I was heavier than him and well planted in a strong stance. As he moved he dropped his guard and I caught him with a reverse punch to the head. I was the first Shotokan Karate International World Kumite Champion!

Two interesting aspects occur to me. Before the final I was talking to a team-mate who is very good at *mae-geri* and I remarked that I very rarely used it, as I didn't feel comfortable with it, although I often visualized it. Yet this is the very kick that I used to level the score. The other point is that because I had spent so much time in keeping calm and treating each match as just another fight, it seemed to take a lifetime before I could feel the excitement of being a world champion. I was still subconsciously keeping myself calm and relaxed.

# Chapter 16 **COACHING**

## The aim

The coach's aim is to improve the effectiveness of his student. In sport karate terms it can be subdivided into two main aspects:

(1) Analysis of current specific skills and developing routines to improve or enhance them on a regular on-going basis (short-term and long-term goal setting).

(2) Preparing the student psychologically and physically for the demands of competition by (a) ensuring that the student approaches the event in peak mental and physical condition, and (b) by acting as technical adviser and psychological support during the event itself.

It goes without saying that the coach must be an experienced competitor in his or her own right and must also be fully aware of the advances in knowledge of body mechanics, kinesiology, anatomy, sport medicine, sport psychology and the like.

*Kanazawa coaching at Nottingham University*

A good coach must be a good analyser. He or she must be able to view critically and analyse both overall and specific skills in each individual student – for example, the overall lack of mobility as compared with a minor element such as forgetting to guard the face when reverse punching. The coach must realize that unlike teaching in a normal class situation, each student will have individual requirements which will necessitate long-term goal setting and the planning of training schedules specifically related to the particular fault to be eradicated or skill to be enhanced.

The step from instructor to coach is a big one. The coach must gain an intimate knowledge of the physical skills and the psychological make-up of each of the students. Each will respond differently to the stresses of training and competition, and each will require a different form of motivation. Some will respond to shouts and threats, others will need praise. Each athlete is different and the coach will need to be fully aware of these differences and know exactly how to apply the pressure or ease off as the situation demands.

Research into the 'coaching personality' indicates that in general the most common characteristics are: a dominant personality, well organized, good at forward planning, likes to be on top; basically emotionally stable under stress, and having good leadership qualities, readily accepting responsibility; a stubborn tenacious nature, generally in sympathy with the normal social values. On the negative side, this 'coaching personality' also displays a tendency towards inflexibility and the inability to comprehend fully or sympathise with the need for psychological support in those not so self-sufficient.

Although the karate coach is a relatively new phenomenon it is by no means impossible to develop a karate-specific programme using the coach's karate knowledge in conjunction with knowledge and expertise gained by the many years of experience in the coaching of other sports.

In Great Britain the National Coaching Foundation was established to provide a service for coaches of all sports, and has devised a series of study packs on a number of topics analysing:

(1) What is the coach's job? *The Coach In Action*.
(2) Fitness and how it is achieved: *The Body in Action*.
(3) Preventing injury and coping with accidents: *Safety and Injury*.
(4) How to analyse movement: *Improving Techniques*.
(5) Understanding behaviour: *Mind over Matter*.
(6) Organizing training sessions and schedules: *Planning and Practice*.

These introductory study packs can be followed up by attending mini-courses of some four to six hours' duration on these and other allied topics such as: 'The Use of Video in Sport', 'Understanding

*Two of Great Britain's finest coaches, 'Ticky' Donovan and Billy Higgins, in Madrid*

and Improving Skill', 'How to Plan Your Programme' 'Development of Strength and Speed'. These and other courses, designed and presented by experts in their particular fields, will form a basis of eclectic knowledge from which a personal karate-centred programme can be constructed. (The NCF's address can be found in the Appendix. Our association, the Federation of Shotokan Karate, encourages all our instructors, and indeed senior students, to attend these courses, so useful are they.)

Unlike the field of athletics, karate is only now beginning to realize the value of top-class coaching. Indeed, some of the very best world champion *karate-ka*, such as Jeoff Thompson, have had to look outside karate to the world of athletics for a competent coach. Some of this apparent apathy stems from the continual political skirmishing which has gone on over the years between the different karate organizations. This has meant that it has seldom if ever been possible in the last ten years to form a truly representative national squad and pay for the necessary services of a full-time coach.

The British team has performed magnificently and the number of gold medals won by it and its individual members confirms Great Britain as one of the finest karate nations in the world. All too often, however, the *karate-ka* have been let down by the politicians. Until the political differences are resolved, and proper structured coaching programmes instituted which are recognized and supported by all the various bodies, it will still be left to each individual to draw support – financial and coaching – from wherever possible.

Another factor in this apparent reluctance in accepting the importance of the coach is the deeply held assumption by some that karate, not being truly a sport, would somehow be diminished by contributions from purely sporting areas of concern such as track and field. The short-sightedness of this type of thinking has been discussed elsewhere. Fortunately this attitude is changing and common sense is beginning to prevail. In the end we must agree with Francis Bacon: 'Knowledge itself is power' (*Religious Meditations*).

One of the areas in which a coach must specialize is that of organizing. Most *karate-ka* and indeed most fighters will have a good general understanding of good – as opposed to bad – training sessions or what to be aware of in general terms in an opponent. The coach, however, must analyse and organize this general understanding until specifics emerge. To take just one example: in competition the coach should know in advance the different strategies which would be used to bring his particular fighters to the contest arena in top physical and mental shape, but in order to define the correct tactical approach for each fighter he should also have analysed the opposition in the same way.

Of course, at club and minor level this is simply impossible, but at higher-level events the coach should be familiar with the styles of the likely opposition: Are there any favourite or speciality techniques to watch out for and be ready to

counter? Is the opponent a 'one-pace' fighter to be hustled out of his natural rhythm? Is the opponent an attacker or counter attacker, using flashy or basic technique? Does he start slowly and warm up or charge straight in? and so on. All these considerations should have been assessed and strategies and tactics developed which should have formed the basis of mental rehearsal and visualization routines well before the event, so that the coach's fighters can go on to the mat knowing in advance the likely course of the match.

Even at this stage, however, a coach can be invaluable in giving the correct mat-side advice and encouragement. During the course of a karate match there are many instances where natural breaks occur, during which a fighter could be reminded of any particular tactic which he might have overlooked in the heat of the moment, or he could be given some indication of a weakness in his opponent which would appear to have escaped his attention. The coach should also have an intimate knowledge of the rules of the competition, and should be there to protect his fighters from any infringements.

Finally, the coach has the duty of organizing the after-match wind-down. He should have recorded the successes and failures of his fighters, and helped them to fill in the post-contest psychological assessment forms, upon which he can base his future strategies and preparation schedules.

*Aidan sparring with English National coach T. Donovan, Amsterdam 1981*

In the field of athletics it has been found that coaching is an intensely personal thing, often carried out on a one-to-one basis. It is more than likely that this will also be the most effective method of coaching in karate. Unlike athletics, however, the coach must remember that there is a philosophical side to karate and that he must always have in the back of his mind the realization that life at the top in sport karate is of relatively short duration, and the karate competitor must be continually reminded that there is a lifetime of karate training beyond the narrow confines of *shiai-jo* (competition area).

What must remain true for both the coach and the instructor is that the whole objective of teaching is for the student eventually to surpass the master! If this does not happen then something is wrong, and if the student never betters the performance of his or her teacher, then the skill level of the sport or art as a whole must inevitably decline as the process continues when the student in time becomes a teacher.

With this in mind, the coach must always be wary of encouraging look-a-like clones. By their very nature they will be only poor copies of the original, never even their equal. Imitation is flattering, and of course right from the start we ask our students to watch and imitate our techniques. Eventually, however, every student must be pushed, coerced, persuaded – whatever – into finding his own way forward and realizing his own potential.

Particularly in 'traditional' schools maintaining the emphasis on the 'way' of karate, the serious student must at some time have all emotional and psychological 'band-aids' removed in order to help him plumb the depths of his own psyche and look at himself and his strengths and weaknesses with a clear, uncluttered vision.

# Chapter 17 THE FEDERATION OF SHOTOKAN KARATE

The Federation was formed in 1986 with the aim of furthering, promoting and developing the knowledge, understanding and dissemination of Shotokan karate. This is to be achieved essentially by basing training upon tried and tested traditional methods of discipline and rigorous physical practice, but incorporating also the modern techniques and approaches to physical fitness developed by research in sport medicine and bio-mechanics.

## The chief instructor

Aidan Trimble brings impressive qualifications to his role as Chief Instructor. A long-time student of Shiro Asano 7th dan, Aidan has trained with many of the finest teachers in both 'traditional' and 'sport' karate.

Aidan's list of achievements is simply too long to detail here, but in passing it is worth noting that while in the Shotokan Karate International he was:

three times British Individual Champion
three times British Team Champion
four times Asano Shield Team Champion
three times Kata Champion
twice European Team Champion
British All-Students Individual Champion
Twice England All-Styles Kata Champion
The first World Individual Kumite Champion, winning the title in Tokyo

Aidan also has a wide knowledge of other sports, and as Nottinghamshire's county karate coach is well known for his friendly and instructive talks and demonstrations to both schools and the business community in Nottinghamshire. He is also coach for the all-styles county karate squad.

As well as being a professional karate instructor, Aidan has acted as a consultant to TV and film companies for action scenes.

## Assistant chief instructor

Vince Morris came to Nottingham University in 1969 with nine years' judo experience behind him. He became a student of Shiro Asano 7th dan, training regularly with him for the next twelve years. During his stay at the University, Vince became chief instructor of the karate club, leading the University team on to win the British Universities Championships. As an individual fighter he also became a successful member of the British Universities International Team.

As an SKI member, Vince was three times British Team Champion and twice runner-up. Also a *kata* medallist, Vince was a member of the winning international squad at European level in both *kumite* and *kata*. He is also a qualified referee.

On the political scene Vince established the English Karate Federation, and following a period as Vice-chairman he went on to become the Chairman of the Martial Arts Commission, the governing body for all martial arts. The author of one of the best-selling books on karate, *The Karate-dō Manual*, Vince brings to the Federation a wide experience in other sports. He is also a successful businessman and lecturer.

Both Aidan and Vince are in demand to teach in Britain and abroad, not just by Shotokan groups but by organizations of many different styles. The Federation encourages its instructors to participate in the courses arranged by the National Coaching Foundation, and also provides regular free courses for its black and brown belt students.

In line with its aim of promoting the practice of karate as a means of self-awareness and development, the Federation encourages its members to do as much as they are able towards creating a better society, both by example and by effort. The Federation is very proud of the example

*Dirk Robertson and student*

set by black belt Dirk Robertson in using his karate-dō knowledge in helping the mentally and physically disadvantaged to achieve a dignity, control and self-confidence hitherto denied them, and would ask all *karate-ka* in every style and organization to follow his example in giving something back to society.

Anyone wishing to correspond with either Aidan or Vince can do so by writing to:

The Federation of Shotokan Karate
PO Box 47
West PDO
Nottingham NG8 2EA

# APPENDIX

For those who would like to read further on some of the subjects dealt with in this book, we recommend the following books and magazines:

## Books

*Athletic Ability and the Anatomy of Motion*, Rolf Wirhead (Wolf Medical Publications, London).

*Hara: The Vital Centre of Man*, K. G. von Durkheim (A Mandala Book, Unwin Paperbacks, London).

*Hardcore Bodybuilding*, Robert Kennedy (Sterling Publishing Co. Inc, New York).

*The Karate-dō Manual*, P. M. V. (Vince) Morris (Stanley Paul & Co. Ltd, London).

*Maximum Sports Performance*, James F. Fixx (Angus & Robertson Ltd, London).

*Psyching for Sport*, Terry Orlick (Leisure Press, Illinois, USA).

*The Pursuit of Sporting Excellence*, David Hemery (Collins Willow Ltd, London).

*Sporting Body, Sporting Mind*, John Syer and Christopher Donnolly (Cambridge University Press).

*Transcendental Meditation*, Bloomfield, Cain & Jaffe (Unwin Paperbacks, London).

*The Way of Karate Beyond Technique*, Shigeru Egami (Ward Lock Ltd, London).

*Zen for Beginners*, J. Blackstone and Z. Josipovic (Unwin Paperbacks, London).

*Zen and the Ways*, T. P. Leggett (Routledge & Kegan Paul, London).

*Zen Training*, Katsuki Sekida (Weatherhill, New York, Tokyo).

## Magazines

*American Karate*, Ed. David Weiss, 351 West 54th Street, New York, NY 10019, USA.

*Combat*, Ed. Mike Haig, 135 Aldridge Road, Perry Barr, Birmingham B42 2ET.

*Fighting Arts International*, Ed. Terry O'Neill, PO Box 26, Birkenhead, Merseyside L43 4YQ.

*Martial Arts Illustrated*, Ed. Bob Sykes, Revenue Chambers, St Peters Street, Huddersfield HD1 1DL.

*Shotokan Karate Magazine*, Ed. John Cheetham, 1 Grove Court, Lymm, Cheshire.

*Traditional Karate*, Ed. Mike Haig, 99 John Bright Street, Birmingham B1 1BE.

## Useful Addresses

The Federation of Shotokan Karate, PO Box 47, West PDO, Nottingham NG8 2EA.

The National Coaching Foundation, 4 College Close, Beckett Park, Leeds LS6 3QH.